ADVISOR PREP® SERIES

MULTIPLE MINI INTERVIEW
FOR THE MIND

2017-2018 EDITION

KEVYN TO M.D

Printed in the United States of America

Second Edition, 2017

ISBN-13: 9781635878400

APE Advisor Prep
20 Trafalgar Square
Suite 464
Nashua, NH 03063
Toll Free: 1-844-999-PREP (7737)

Visit us online at:
https://apetest.com/edu
and
http://mminterview.com

Dedications

"... to all aspiring applicants. May **God**
Bless you in your endeavors."

Acknowledgments

> "Thank you to all of our students for their invaluable input and support"

Disclaimer

This book is presented solely for educational purposes. The publisher is not offering it as legal, or professional services advice. While best efforts have been used in preparing this book, the publisher makes no representations or warranties of any kind and assumes no liabilities of any kind with respect to the accuracy or completeness of the contents. The publisher shall not be held liable or responsible to any person or entity with respect to any loss or incidental or consequential damages caused, or alleged to have been caused, directly or indirectly, by the information contained herein. References when provided are for informational purposes only and do not constitute endorsement of any websites or other sources. Please be aware that the websites listed in this book may change. This book is not intended as a substitute for personalized Multiple Mini Interview or CASPer® preparation provided by APE Advisor Prep®.

APE Advisor Prep® is not affiliated with, nor endorsed by the CASPer® test, Altus Assessments or any program/institution.

*conditions apply for rank better and score higher claim.

TABLE OF CONTENTS

(this page is intentionally left blank)

Welcome to APE
Multiple Mini Interview for the Mind

Are you ready to master the Multiple Mini Interview? Advisor Prep® Education (APE) has been helping applicants just like you excel on their Multiple Mini Interview (MMInterview) shortly after the MMInterview made its debut at the McMaster University, Michael G. DeGroote School of Medicine over 10 years ago. The MMInterview has since gained widespread adoption at leading medical schools worldwide and continues to be the interview format of choice at a growing number of medical schools. A great performance on the MMInterview is crucial to receiving the acceptance you're ultimately seeking.

No one understands MMInterview preparation better than APE Advisor Prep®. Our founder, Dr. Kevyn To has been successfully mentoring medical school applicants with their MMInterviews in the United States and Canada for over a decade with unmatched success. Our students feel great after their actual MMInterviews and they're equally thrilled with their success at receiving first round admission offers at these schools and programs.

Before you take the plunge and start preparing for your MMInterview, take a step back and ask yourself the following question: Do you see the MMInterview as an opportunity or a barrier towards your ultimate goal of being admitted to your top choice program? If you answered the *latter*, we encourage you to immediately change your outlook and embrace every opportunity to control your performance and to sell your personal and professional characteristics to your desired schools and programs.

How should I use this book?

Congratulations on taking the first and most important step towards mastering your MMinterviews. Multiple Mini Interview for the Mind is the world's best-selling MMInterview guide and for the 2017-2018 edition, we've included a number of revolutionary features such as online video response scoring with our Multiple Mini Indicator (MMI®) Score for all books purchased directly through the APE Advisor Prep® website.

To get you up and running, we'll walk you through what you need to know (and do) in order to maximize your benefit from this book. **We're going to help you rank better on your MMInterview*.** This book was written to provide background information about the MMInterview and to act as a companion to APE Director, Inconel™ and Insider students' personalized on-one-one MMInterview preparation. However, even if you are not signed up with one of these programs, you'll still benefit from the pearls, tips and framework provided in this book. The expert answer discussions to the MMInterview scenarios are designed to act as a springboard to help you brainstorm and arrive towards your own effective answers for your interview.

After you've finished reading the first ten chapters, you should go online to apetest.com to submit your video response to the baseline scenario from chapter 11 and receive your MMI® Score. To do this, you'll need the redemption code provided in this back of your book. If you didn't purchase your copy directly from APE Advisor Prep®, we still encourage you to participate for a small additional fee. As you work through the book, we suggest that you come up with your own answers to each of the scenarios, prior to examining the sample model answers provided.

To get the most out of this book, we've included the following checklist:

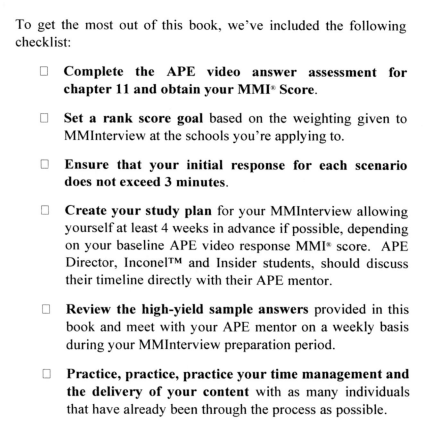

- ☐ **Complete the APE video answer assessment for chapter 11 and obtain your MMI® Score.**

- ☐ **Set a rank score goal** based on the weighting given to MMInterview at the schools you're applying to.

- ☐ **Ensure that your initial response for each scenario does not exceed 3 minutes.**

- ☐ **Create your study plan** for your MMInterview allowing yourself at least 4 weeks in advance if possible, depending on your baseline APE video response MMI® score. APE Director, Inconel™ and Insider students, should discuss their timeline directly with their APE mentor.

- ☐ **Review the high-yield sample answers** provided in this book and meet with your APE mentor on a weekly basis during your MMInterview preparation period.

- ☐ **Practice, practice, practice your time management and the delivery of your content** with as many individuals that have already been through the process as possible.

We have designed the book with the APE Advisor Prep student in mind and therefore rationales for select specific model answers have been omitted. These answer rationales are discussed during one-on-one sessions for APE Director, Inconel™ and Insider students and select A-la-carte APE MMI® testing sessions.

Multiple Mini Interview
Fundamentals

01: Introduction to the MMInterview

As an applicant to medical school, an envelope conveniently appeared in Dr. Kevyn To's mailbox from McMaster University on the same day his nephew was born. He couldn't ask for better news. He was once again an uncle and the letter from McMaster University had informed him that he had been carefully selected to participate in an on-campus interview for the undergraduate M.D. medical program. The interview package also contained information about an optional pilot activity called the Multiple Mini Interviews.

The Multiple Mini Interview has been used continuously since 2001.

At the time, the M.D. program's formal interview day consisted of three activities: watching a video followed by a written essay response, participating in an observed group activity and finally the dreaded panel interview.

Using MMInterviews in the medical school admissions' process was unheard of over a decade ago and the concept of multiple mini interviews replacing traditional interviews was still in its infancy. The idea of staying behind after an already long interview day to be a guinea pig was not very enticing but he decided to be a good sport about it. Looking back, the opportunity to participate in the pilot MMInterviews at McMaster University, prior to their current widespread use worldwide has allowed him to gain a unique perspective on their initial development as an assessment tool and how they continue to shape the admissions process to medical schools around the globe.

A common learning approach in medicine has been to "See one. Do one. Teach one." However, when it comes to interviewing for medical school, applicants are still continually told to "just be themselves" and to skip out on any formal MMInterview preparation. Picture yourself among a sea of qualified applicants with stellar GPAs and MCAT scores. Ask yourself the following question truthfully.

The majority of programs using the Multiple Mini Interview, do not provide applicants with a clipboard and paper to write down their thoughts beforehand.

"Can you realistically distinguish yourself from other highly qualified applicants by just being yourself?"

Medical school admissions committees are fully aware that the interview is potentially the biggest game changer for any qualified applicant and this is the fundamental reason why the MMInterviews came into existence. In addition to academic achievement, medical schools value an unbiased admission's process that can select for applicants with strong interpersonal skills, integrity and professionalism [1].

Recognizing that traditional interviews are subject to context and evaluator bias, the MMInterviews were adapted from the objective structured clinical examination (OSCE) to try and minimize interview bias [2]. The rationale for MMInterviews is that compared with traditional interviews, testing an array of domains of competency, each with a different interviewer, avoids bias attributable to context specificity [3].

As previous assessors of the MMInterviews at leading medical schools in the United States and Canada, APE mentors continue to see their widespread acceptance and implementation by many health programs. From their inception into the McMaster University, School of Medicine's MD program admissions process to widespread

For the Multiple Mini Interview, it's not just what you say but also how you say it that matters.

use worldwide, the MMInterviews have been subject to much scrutiny and validation. Systematic reviews continue to validate that MMInterviews are reliable and statistically predictive of subsequent performance at national medical licensing exams [4]. Their use in the admissions' selection process will only continue to grow.

Depending on the specific program where you interview, your MMInterview circuit will likely consist of 6 to 12 stations and may include rest stations. There will be as many participants in your interview circuit as there are stations.

The instructions for each station are typically posted directly outside of each room and you are given up to two minutes to carefully read the prompt prior to entering the room. At the end of the two minutes, a bell will sound and this is your queue to enter the room. Typically, a bell ringer type method is used to keep track of the time and you will be allocated six to eight minutes for each station before moving on to the next station.

During each encounter, you will be expected to complete a task and for most stations, the interviewer will follow up with a standardized set of probing questions to engage you in further discussion. Some programs will provide you with blank paper and a clipboard to write down your thoughts but the vast majority of programs will not. Our suggestion is to work through your interview preparation with the assumption that you will not be able to take notes.

The types of MMInterview stations you'll encounter on interview day can essentially be grouped into one of the following categories:

1) **Ethical Stations**

2) **Cultural Competency Stations**

3) **Social Issues/Health Policy Stations**

4) **Role Playing Stations**

5) **Collaboration Stations**

6) **Traditional Interview Stations**

7) **Writing Stations**

8) **Video Stations**

9) **Rest Stations**

We'll explore each category in more detail.

Ethical stations will describe a common scenario whereby a fundamental ethical principle is at risk or has been violated and require you to identify and discuss important issues around that ethical principle as it applies to that scenario. The fundamental ethical principles are beneficence, do no harm, justice, autonomy and consent.

Cultural Competency stations assess your ability to recognize the cultural characteristics deemed important in order to successfully practice medicine in the school's geographic environment and beyond. They often describe an emotionally charged scenario and require you to identify and explore the pertinent issues. Example topics may include racism, gender bias, elder abuse, mental health, gay marriage, gay adoption and legalization of marijuana.

Social Issues & Health Policy stations typically assess your ability to recognize common barriers to the practice of medicine as relevant to the school's geographic environment and beyond.

They may include scenarios on limited access to care in rural health, abortion or increased wait times to see a specialist. These scenarios may share commonalities with ethical stations but should not be lumped into the same category.

Role Playing (Acting) stations tend to be the most difficult for many applicants because of their artificial nature. They often involve an actor or standardized patient. Be prepared to complete a common task such as delivering bad news, confronting a person about a problem or gathering information from the individual. The interviewer will act as an observer present in the room to assess your language, demeanor and effectiveness at completing the task.

Collaboration stations require working with another co-applicant or more recently, directly with the interviewer to complete a specified task. One applicant provides the instructions while the other receives them. You may be positioned back to back and blinded to each other. These scenarios may involve a drawing, a math problem, and a series of images or a phone conversation. In all cases, you are required to complete a given task using only verbal communication and your interaction will be assessed by an interviewer in the room. The frequency of collaboration stations on MMInterview circuits has increased dramatically over the last few years. As a result, we've dedicated an entire separate chapter to mastering these types of MMInterview stations.

Traditional Interview stations are self-explanatory and designed to gain insight into who you are and your motivations for selecting a specific health profession and the particular school you are interviewing for. These have grown more popular over the last 3 years. They generally require you to answer one or more questions such as "Why medicine? Why did you apply to this medical school? What are your weaknesses? etc."

Essay Writing stations require you to articulate your thoughts on paper within a restricted time interval. These stations have become even rarer over the last few years. When they do appear, they are usually 15-20 minutes in length. These stations do not require any verbal communication input. We will not explore essay writing stations any further in this book.

Video stations require you to watch a short clip often less than 90 seconds. The video often highlights a type of relationship and generally revolves around a conflict/disagreement. You will not be able to replay the clip so pay close attention. Afterwards, you are required to articulate pertinent details of the interaction to your interviewer succinctly and engage in standardized probing questions. These types of stations have fallen out of use significantly over the past 3 years and will not be explored any further in this book.

Rest stations allow you the opportunity to refresh and recharge. The MMInterview circuit is fast paced and requires a lot of concentration and energy. Since you are generally not allowed to leave the circuit, you cannot use the rest station as a bathroom break. However, refresher beverages and snacks are usually present at rest stations. Use rest stations as an opportunity to clear your mind and to get ready for the next station instead of dwelling on your performance from previous stations.

The nine categories may seem overwhelming as you prepare for your MMInterviews because in theory they allow for an endless combination of stations. However, in reality there are only a finite number of personal characteristics assessed. It is crucial that you remember this fact.

References

1. Eva KW, et. al. An Admissions OSCE: The multiple mini interview. Medical Education 2004; 38: 314–326

2. Cameron AJ, et al. Development and Pilot Testing of a Multiple Mini-Interview for Admission to a Pharmacy Degree Program. Am J Pharm Educ. 2012 February 10; 76(1):10.

3. Eva KW, et al. The ability of the multiple mini interview to predict preclerkship performance in medical school. Acad Med. 2004;79(10 Suppl):S40–S42.

4. Eva KW, et. al. Association between a medical school admission process using the multiple mini-interview and national licensing examination scores. JAMA. 2012 Dec 5;308(21):2233-40

02: MMInterview & CASPer®

As we previously eluded to, medical schools and affiliated health professional programs evaluate personal and professional qualities in their applicants. Traditionally, this has presented challenges because the current admission models were unable to assess these characteristics with any reliability.

The CASPer® test uses **open ended questions** just like the Multiple Mini Interview to capture a broader range of answers from examinees.

In addition to academic achievement, medical schools, and other allied health professional programs value applicants with strong interpersonal attributes, integrity, trust, empathy and professionalism. This lead to the creation of the Multiple Mini Interview which is currently the preferred interview format used to screen candidates at many programs in Canada and the United States.

Fast forward several years and the same team at McMaster University has applied the concept of the MMInterview towards a pre-interview assessment tool. *CASPer® is essentially an online MMInterview test that is being rapidly adopted at medical schools and professional health programs around the world.*

Similar to the MMInterview, applicants are left in the dark about their CASPer® test performance and often mislead into believing that preparation and practice is not required nor beneficial. At certain medical school programs, the MMInterview and CASPer® are weighted equally, each totaling approximately 35% of the admissions outcome.

The CASPer® test is essentially an **online 90 minute Multiple Mini Interview** consisting of twelve, 5 minute stations.

Proper time management is essential for both the CASPer® test and the MMInterview. You'll want to allow yourself 30 seconds prior to the end of your MMInterview station to reiterate any main points made or clarify any loose ends and finish on your best foot.

03: MMInterview Facts & Myths

In this chapter, we'll focus on the most common widely held facts and myths surrounding the MMInterviews. Applicants to medical, dental, pharmacy, veterinary schools etc. come in all shapes and sizes with a huge variety of background experiences. Most schools are not interested in further assessing your academic background at the interview stage using the MMInterviews. This is worth remembering as you prepare and reinforces that the MMInterviews are used to assess personal qualities and increasingly for professional characteristics.

To minimize the effects of rater fatigue, schedule your interview in the morning if possible.

#1: MMInterviews evaluate applicants on their subject based knowledge.

This is a Myth.

Whether you major in music or chemistry, your specific knowledge base in a particular subject will not be tested or evaluated.

#2: MMInterviews evaluate applicants on their clinical based knowledge.

This is a Myth.

An applicant with a nursing degree will not have an unfair advantage over an applicant with a law degree. Clinical knowledge includes, but is not limited to knowledge of events such as examining, diagnosing, counseling or managing patient specific medical conditions, concerns, or outcomes.

To minimize the effect of rater bias on your Multiple Mini Interview score, avoid volunteering your opinion on controversial topics. Focus your answers around your personal experiences instead.

#3: MMInterviews evaluate your ability to correctly and promptly follow instructions.

This is a Fact.

A common reason why applicants receive lower scores is due to the fact they overlook simple directions. For example, if the scenario requires you to **discuss** your answer, then make sure you accomplish this instead of just **stating** your answer. We will have a lot more to say about this point as we work through specific examples.

Did you know that typically anyone within the community without a conflict of interest can sign up to be a MMInterviewer.

#4: MMInterviews assess your ability to communicate effectively and efficiently in the time allocated.

This is a Fact.

Self-explanatory and remember that non-verbal communication is also assessed.

#5: MMInterviewers expect applicants to present and discuss all aspects of conflicting viewpoints.

This is a Myth.

Each station is bound by very specific time constraints. As a result, an applicant will not be able to effectively present and discuss all relevant aspects to a MMInterview station. We will discuss how to selectively discuss the most relevant viewpoints throughout the book.

If there are fewer than 3 weeks before your actual interview, don't panic. Be sure to familiarize yourself with the logistics of the interview and focus on the characteristics assessed as presented in the subsequent chapters.

#6: MMInterviews evaluate your ability to apply general working knowledge to issues relevant to the culture/society in which you live.

This is a Fact.

Your MMInterviewers are trained to evaluate how well you can apply common working knowledge of your culture/society into your decision making process. Although not explicitly assessed, one of the key challenges is to learn how to make yourself memorable to the interviewer. Strategies for doing so will be discussed in subsequent chapters as we tackle specific examples.

#7: MMInterviews evaluate your ability to think critically on the spot.

This is a Fact.

Your MMInterviewers will assess your ability to respond critically to different scenarios. Thinking on the spot is often thought to be an innate skill, but like any skill, the secret is to learn how to make the mind more comfortable with the task by establishing a prepared framework to build your thoughts around. Once your mind is comfortable with the structure, it's easy to fill in the gaps. Fortunately with the MMInterviews, there are only a finite number of personal and professional characteristics being assessed.

#8: MMInterviews evaluate your ability to defend and discuss your personal opinions.

This is a Fact.

As a practicing physician, dentist, pharmacist, veterinarian or allied health professional, you will constantly be challenged about your choices and the decision process behind those choices. The MMInterviews will try to simulate this so it is important to have an opinion, stick to your guns and **not flip flop or sit on the fence**.

#9: It is acceptable to make small talk with the MMInterviewer if you finish your station early.

This is a Myth.

Do not engage in small talk if you finish early. We will discuss what to do in these situations subsequently.

#10: MMInterviews do not have a right or wrong answer.

This is a Myth.

For each MMInterview, there may exist many unacceptable answers as well as multiple strong, acceptable answers. You've likely heard of the euphemism, "there's more than one way to skin a cat." The same applies to the MMInterview.

04: Benefits of the MMInterview

Prior to adopting a Multiple Mini Interview format, each program must evaluate the benefits and consequences of abandoning the long favored traditional interview format.

Research shows that performance on behavioral interviews like the MMInterview are enhanced with advance practice and preparation.

To do so, schools and programs resort to the growing mound of evidence in research literature surrounding the MMInterview's increased reliability in selecting applicants for specific personal characteristics.

Broadly speaking, the current benefits of the MMInterview format can be summarized into direct benefits for the administering program and for individual applicants.

MMInterview - Direct Applicant Benefits

> **Greater Number of First Impressions**
> **Greater Fairness and Transparency**
> **Greater Faculty Engagement & Exposure**
> **Greater Number of Independent Encounters**

MMInterview - Direct Program Benefits

When preparing for the Multiple Mini Interview, create a diary of relevant personal experiences.

> **Greater Reliability and Validity**
> **Fewer Interviewer Biases**
> **Greater Flexibility in screening for desired traits**
> **Greater Number of Candidates can be screened**

05: Reapplicants & the MMInterview

Each year, thousands of highly qualified medical school applicants are rejected post MMInterview. To throw some salt into their wounds, the majority of these applicants receive little to no feedback on their interview performance, leaving them with little knowledge of where things went wrong. Desperate for strategies for improvement, many of these applicants resort to premed forums and are often forced to rely on information from unknown sources. This is compounded by the fact that schools and programs may mislead applicants directly by recommending that they not prepare in advance for their MMInterviews. However, the truth is advanced preparation is essential to ensuring a strong performance on the MMInterview because with the time constraints imposed, the majority of applicants will require advanced practice to become comfortable and skilled with the process.

Statistics shows that over 25% of current medical students were reapplicants.

In the process, applicants often overlook a key element that may ultimately contribute to their rejection: a lack of self-reflection. Research on the MMInterview shows that if you are rejected post interview, your best chances of improving are by reflecting on the scenarios and stations you encountered. In one research study by *B. Griffin et al.*, candidates who repeated their MMInterview the following year after having been unsuccessful the previous year showed an increase in scores on stations that were either the same as or similar to previous stations.

Applicants who are unsuccessful initially, typically lack adequate interview preparation.

With self-reflection and the proper guidance, all applicants will benefit from advance preparation for their MMInterviews.

06: Changing MMInterview Landscape

Over the past decade, APE Advisor Prep® has worked with countless students seeking admission to a wide range of health professional programs inside and outside of medicine. Based on our experience, we've noted a drastic change in the landscape of the Multiple Mini Interview in terms of the programs implementing this interview format, the content of the MMInterview stations and MMInterviewer expectations.

We've found that the MMInterviews have shifted in the following ways:

1. **More programs are abandoning video based MMInterview stations.** Video Stations typically require an interviewee to watch a short clip often less than 90 seconds. The video often highlights a type of relationship, its dynamics and generally revolves around a conflict/disagreement. Afterwards, the interviewee is required to articulate pertinent details of the interaction to the interviewer succinctly and engage in standardized probing questions. These stations have fallen out of use significantly over the last 3 years.

2. **More programs are adopting collaboration based MMInterview stations.** Collaboration stations require working with another co-applicant or more recently, directly with the interviewer to complete a specified task. These scenarios may involve a drawing, a math problem, and a series of images or a phone conversation. The frequency of collaboration stations on MMInterview circuits has increased dramatically over the past several years.

3. **More programs are adopting a shorter MMInterview circuit.** At the majority of programs that have implemented the MMInterview over the past 3 years, we've seen a decrease in the total number MMInterview stations per interview circuit. This is most likely due to a combination of factors such as individual program resources and research literature which suggests that a 4-6 station MMInterview can be just as reliable as a longer MMInterview circuit.

4. **More programs across all health professional disciplines are adopting the MMInterview.** With approximately 33% of medical schools in the United States, 80% of medical schools in Canada, 80% of medical schools in the UK favoring this interview model, it's no surprise that other programs have followed suit. Over the past 3 years, we've seen the MMInterview make its way over to just about every possible health discipline you can think of.

5. **More programs are assessing for professionalism directly within the MMInterview.** Research has shown that the majority of medical complaints against providers are due to professionalism rather than medical expert. As a result, over the past several years, many programs have begun to directly assess an applicant's professionalism during the MMInterview in addition to their personal characteristics.

6. **More programs are giving increased weight to an applicant's MMInterview performance.** There has been a noticeable shift in the weighting of the MMInterview at most programs across the globe. For example, the MMInterview now accounts for 70% of the post interview decision at McMaster University, School of Medicine (significantly more than even the MCAT®).

The reasons for these changes are likely multifactorial but related to the fact that the type of applicant deemed desirable to admissions committees has changed in favor of individuals with more to offer outside of stellar GPAs and MCAT scores. In addition, the interview process itself has become more data driven which typically favors applicants with more enriching life experiences, capable of sharing their personal characteristics.

Despite these changes to the landscape of the MMInterview, applicants should not lose focus of their goal of being a competent, caring and compassionate health care provider. If at the end of your MMInterview station, you leave the interviewer with the impression that he or she would approve of having you as a colleague, then you will be well on your way to becoming a doctor.

07: Schools Using the MMInterview

As of 2017, the following schools and programs worldwide have adopted the MMInterview or are in the process of adopting the MMInterview.

Medical School	Country
Albany Medical College	USA
AT Still University	USA
Australian National University	Australia
Brighton and Sussex Medical School	UK
California Northstate University	USA
Cardiff University	UK
Central Michigan University	USA
Dalhousie University	Canada
Deakin University	Australia

Medical School	Country
Duke University	USA
Griffith University	Australia
Hull York Medical School	UK
Keele University	UK
King's College London	UK
Marian University	USA
McMaster University	Canada
McGill University	Canada
Memorial University of Newfoundland	Canada
Michigan State University – DO program	USA
Michigan State University – MD program	USA
Monash University	Australia

Medical School	Country
Newcastle University	UK
New York Medical College	USA
New York University	USA
Northern Ontario Medical School	Canada
Oregon Health & Science University	USA
Pacific Northwest University of Health Sciences	USA
Queen's University - Belfast	UK
Queen's University	Canada
Rosalind Franklin University of Medicine & Sci.	USA
Rutger's University - RWJMS	USA
San Juan Bautista School of Medicine	USA
Stanford University	USA

Medical School	Country
SUNY Upstate	USA
Tufts University	USA
Tulane University	USA
University of Aberdeen	UK
University of Alabama	USA
University of Alberta	Canada
University of Arizona - Phoenix	USA
University of Arizona – Tucson	USA
University of Birmingham	UK
University of Bristol	UK
University of British Columbia	Canada
University of Calgary	Canada

Medical School	Country
University of California – Davis	USA
University of California – Los Angeles	USA
University of California – Riverside	USA
University of California – San Diego	USA
Universidad Central del Caribe	USA
University of Cincinnati	USA
University of Dundee	UK
University of East Anglia	UK
University of Exeter	UK
University of Incarnate Word	USA
University of Lancaster	UK
University of Leeds	UK

Medical School	Country
University of Leicester	UK
University of Liverpool	UK
University of London – St. George's	UK
University of Manchester	UK
University of Massachusetts	USA
University of Melbourne	Australia
University of Michigan	USA
University of Minnesota	USA
University of Mississippi	USA
University of Missouri – Kansas City	USA
University of Nevada – Las Vegas	USA
University of Nevada - Reno	USA

Medical School	Country
University of Notre Dame - Fremantle	Australia
University of Notre Dame - Sydney	Australia
University of Nottingham	UK
University of Puerto Rico	USA
University of Toledo	USA
University of Saskatchewan	Canada
University of Sheffield	UK
University of South Carolina - Greenville	USA
University of St. Andrews	UK
University of Sydney	Australia
University of Texas - Austin	USA
University of Utah	USA

Medical School	Country
University of Vermont	USA
University of Warwick	UK
University of Wollongong	Australia
Université Laval	Canada
Université de Montreal	Canada
Université de Sherbrooke	Canada
Virginia Commonwealth University	USA
Virginia Tech School of Medicine	USA
Washington State University	USA
Wayne State University	USA
Western Michigan University	USA
Western University of Health Sciences	USA

Pharmacy School	Country
Dalhousie University	Canada
Oregon State University	USA
Regis University	USA
Sullivan University	USA
University of Arkansas	USA
University of British Columbia	Canada
University of California – San Francisco	USA
University of Illinois - Chicago	USA
University of Kentucky	USA
University of North Carolina	USA
University of Oklahoma	USA
University of South Florida	USA

Pharmacy School	Country
University of Texas - Austin	USA
University of Texas – El Paso	USA
University of Toronto	Canada

Dental School	Country
AT Still University	USA
LECOM - Florida	USA
Marquette University	USA
Midwestern University	USA
Ohio State University	USA
SUNY – Buffalo	USA
University of Alberta	Canada

University of Michigan	USA
University of Mississippi - Jackson	USA
University of Saskatchewan	Canada
Veterinary Medical Schools	**Country**
Michigan State University	USA
Oregon State University	USA
Texas A&M University	USA
University of Calgary	Canada
University of California - Davis	USA
University of Guelph	Canada
University of Florida	USA
University of Minnesota	USA
Virginia-Maryland Regional College of Vet Med	USA

08: Characteristics Assessed

Traditionally, a lack of professionalism accounts for over **90%** of all complaints in the medical profession. Recently, more emphasis has been placed on assessing professionalism directly in the medical school admissions interview. As part of this heightened awareness, admissions committee are increasingly using the MMInterview to help reduce the number of professionalism based complaints.

Motivation for a medical career is assessed in **98%** of medical school interviews regardless of interview style

Broadly speaking, each MMInterview station is designed to assess between one to three personal characteristics deemed important in becoming a successful, practicing health professional. According to the Association of American Medical Colleges (AAMC) the 10 most commonly assessed personal characteristics during the admissions interview are:

1. **Motivation for a medical career**

2. **Compassion and Empathy**

3. **Personal Maturity**

4. **Oral Communication**

5. **Service Orientation**

6. **Professionalism**

7. **Altruism**

8. **Integrity**

9. **Leadership**

10. **Intellectual Curiosity**

Professionalism and Integrity are assessed in **88%** and **83%** of medical school interviews respectively.

A common question we receive from our students is, *"How will I know which qualities are being tested"*? The short answer is without advance practice, it is often very difficult to develop a gestalt for what qualities are being assessed. However, with the right tools and guidance, this can often be quickly teased out during the initial two minutes as you read the prompt.

Consider the following example; the prompt you are reading describes a role playing situation whereby your best friend has just been dumped by their partner. Your task is to interact with your best friend. Based on the language used in the prompt, it is reasonable to assume that emotions such as *anger, fear, sadness and possibly even confusion* are going to dominate this station. Since you will be dealing with another person's "emotions", it's safe to assume that **compassion and empathy** are going to be heavily assessed. As we walk through the book, we'll spend time discussing how to show these two traits in your interview. We'll also point out exactly how to recognize and predict which qualities are being assessed within your MMInterview station.

Finally, as the majority of MMInterviews are largely situation based, it is crucial that you always refer back to your need for self-reflection, and whenever possible during a station, display your overwhelming ability at being an effective *collaborator, communicator, advocate and professional.*

09: MMInterview Scoring

Understanding how you will be assessed during your MMInterview station will help guide your preparation. At APE Advisor Prep®, our proprietary Multiple Mini Indicator (MMI®) Score has been used since 2009 to reliably help many applicants gauge their performance prior to their actual interview. We're thrilled to provide you with your free* MMI® Score as part of our "Better Feedback. Better Results." promise for books purchased directly from us.

We've broken down this chapter into general MMInterviewer scoring guidelines and general MMInterviewee scoring tips.

Remember ASS in your evaluations:

Ability to communicate effectively.

Strength of positions.

Suitability for the program.

Scoring Tips for MMInterviewees

> ➤ **Overall scores are generally assigned from 0 (lowest) to 10 (highest) per station.**

> ➤ **You can generally score poorly on two stations and still receive an outright admissions offer so don't dwell on your performance from past stations.**

> ➤ **Many programs drop your highest station and lowest station scores. The remaining scores are then averaged to obtain your composite interview score.**

> ➤ **Remember to maximize your Ability to communicate effectively, Strength of positions and Suitability for the program.**

Scoring Guidelines for MMInterviewers

> ➤ Each applicant will have two minutes to read the scenario prompt. Do not allow more than two minutes to read the prompt. If the applicant does not enter the room after two minutes, promptly escort them into your room.

> ➤ Start the interview by asking them "if they have had a chance to read the entire prompt?"

> ➤ Do not begin the station until you have verbal confirmation that the applicant has read and understood the station instructions.

> ➤ Do not interrupt the applicant while they are speaking. When they are finished giving their answer, please proceed with the probing questions.

> ➤ At the end of the station, complete the attached evaluation sheets.

> ➤ Assign each score only once per category.

Sample MMInterview Scoring Template

Please rate the applicant's overall performance on this station relative to all applicants you are rating. Do not assign a score more than once (ie. if assessing 10 applicants, you may only use a score of 10 once). You may adjust your scores before submitting.

Consider the applicant's:

        Ability to communicate effectively
        Strength of the arguments displayed
        Suitability for the program

Please place an "X" in the desired box below:

1	2	3	4	5	6	7	8	9	10
Poor			Average				Excellent		

10: KISS IT to Succeed

The MMInterviews are administered under strict timed conditions which makes time management a very important aspect to master when practicing for this interview format. Remember that the most effective answer is going to be the one that delivers your key message within the first two minutes. Any longer and you have likely added unnecessary complexity and this must be avoided. In the 1960s, the U.S. Navy introduced the idea that most systems work best if they are kept simple rather than made complex; therefore simplicity should be a key goal in design. The same holds true for the MMInterviews.

To help you succeed on interview day, we're going to introduce the APE Advisor Prep® K.I.S.S. I.T. (Keep It Short, Simple Interview Training) method for the MMInterviews. It consists of visualizing five pockets with the goal of getting you to reach into your pockets as often as you need to. Before we talk about the pockets, let's review additional MMInterview fundamentals.

Treat each multiple mini interview as a very brief **separate job interview**. Make sure to read each station's prompt and instructions **very carefully**. Be sure to **knock prior** to entering each room. As an evaluator, if an applicant fails to knock prior to entering the room, this will get noted. Once you set foot into the room, please **wait to be seated**. Do not assume it's acceptable for you to just sit down at the closest available seat. Depending on the interviewer's preference, they may or may not shake your hand. Please let them make the first move to shake your hand.

Do not initiate a handshake with the interviewer. Allow them the control in exercising this option with you.

When using a buzz word in your answer, remember to back up your buzz word with personal experience whenever possible.

Do not be the first one to initiate a handshake with the interviewer.

The interviewer will likely start each station by asking if you've had a chance to read the prompt and if there are any questions. In the past, there were applicants rejected post interview who claimed they did not have sufficient time to read the prompts.

Use the first 15-20 seconds of your response time to briefly summarize the scenario to the interviewer. Speak concisely using minimal words and avoid distractions as you are giving your answer. Common distractions include twiddling your fingers, leg shaking, holding objects in your hands or looking at objects in the room while you are speaking. If you are guilty of any of the above, video tape yourself so you can see yourself in action and make the changes accordingly. Deliver your answer with clarity and calmly to ensure that your response can be properly heard and understood by the interviewer. If you have a naturally soft voice, I suggest recording your answers and playing them back to family members or friends to gauge their opinion.

Summarizing the scenario at the beginning provides the interviewer the opportunity to intervene, in case you've incorrectly interpreted key details from the prompt.

Avoid fillers such as "like, uhm, eh" that will take away from your message and avoid using extreme adjectives such as "always, never, absolutely, right, wrong etc" which may be viewed as radical and take away from your answer. In medicine, things are rarely black and white. When the time comes to move on to your next station, remember to leave your chair in the exact position you found it at the beginning. End your station by saying "thank you for your time" to the interviewer.

Your brain is literally creating new neural pathways, much like the interstate highway system, carrying information from one neuron to the next as you read this book. The neurons clump together and are associated with each other as one thing leads you to think of another thing. The process seems disorderly without a conscious framework. Understanding that you learn by doing things over and over again may seem rather intuitive but it is the approach you should take in learning how to master the MMInterviews. From now on, approach each MMInterview scenario you encounter using the following 5 pockets and allow your brain to think in the same framework over and over again.

Do not feel obligated to explore all different perspectives within a scenario. Instead focus on the 2-3 perspectives you are **most comfortable** with.

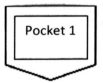

Categorize the MMInterview station into one of the categories presented earlier. Hybrid stations (stations that fit into one or more categories do exist but are less likely) should be prioritized into the category you are most comfortable with. Pocket 1 requires you to ask and answer the following question: *what general category type of scenario is this MMInterview station?*

Identify and acknowledge the main **issue** or problem presented in the MMInterview station. Regardless of the task instructions, this is a key step to establishing a neural pathway to each MMInterview station. Identifying and acknowledging the issue or problem raises awareness within your neuronal networks and will help trigger memories and experiences. Pocket 2 requires you to ask and answer the following question: *what is the main issue or problem in this MMInterview station?*

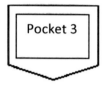

Pocket 3

Identify the main **source** of the problem or issue within the MMInterview station. The goal here is to help you pick out the important concept(s) that you will be evaluated on in the station. Train yourself to get into the habit of picking out the main source of the problem and it will be much easier to spot the concept that is being tested. Pocket 3 requires you to ask and answer the following question: *what is the main source of the issue or problem in this MMInterview station?*

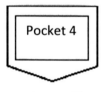

Pocket 4

Identify any relevant **personal experiences** you have that can be incorporated into the MMInterview station. The goal is for you to leave the most positive lasting impression on the interviewer compared to other applicants on your interview circuit. A very effective method of doing so is by using your personal experiences to sell and set yourself apart from the competition. However, please keep in mind that incorporating personal experiences may not be relevant for certain types of MMInterview stations such as role playing. We will illustrate with examples as we work through sample MMInterview stations.

As we talked about during the scoring of MMInterviews, an interviewer must give each applicant a different score. This means that one applicant will receive a 1 and another applicant will receive a 10 if there are ten applicants within the circuit. Pocket 4 requires you to ask and answer the following question: *what personal experiences (if applicable) can I share in my response to help make me the most memorable interviewee for this MMInterview station?*

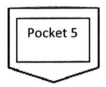

Identify ways to **resolve** or address the problem/issue in the MMInterview station. At this point, you should get into the habit of exploring the main source of the problem or issue from different viewpoints or perspectives. As you do this, it is important to consider the pros and cons from various perspectives. In order to effectively arrive at your answer, you may need to make assumptions. This is absolutely acceptable for the MMInterviews as long as you are transparent and state your assumptions to the interviewer. If used properly, assumptions will highlight to the interviewer your thought process. Pocket 5 requires you to ask and answer the following question: *how would I resolve the problem or issue, taking into account my perspective and other perspectives for this MMInterview station?*

Now that you have your pockets, remember that practice makes perfect. Let's move on to the next chapter and see the APE Advisor Prep KISS IT method in action.

11: APE MMI® Score Assessment

We strongly recommend that you complete your video response assessment to the following station, prior to reading additional chapters in this book. You'll receive your free* APE Advisor Prep Multiple Mini Indicator (MMI®) score which will provide you with a rough idea of your performance relative to other participants.

Multiple Mini Interview: 160221489

STATION INSTRUCTIONS:

You have two minutes to read the scenario below. You will have <u>6 minutes</u> to discuss your answer to the following station below with the interviewer.

You are close friends with Darcy and Mark who have been in a committed relationship with each other for 4 years. An argument between them is now threatening their relationship. Darcy has been offered a promotion as a senior lecturer at a college located 300 miles away and very much wants to accept this position. However, Mark is adamant that Darcy should stay until he finishes his Master's degree and believes that other opportunities will come Darcy's way at such time when they are able to relocate together. Both individuals have confided in you and would like to know your thoughts.

Please discuss with the interviewer any relevant issue(s) related to this situation and what advice you would provide to Darcy and Mark.

Instructions for receiving your APE MMI® Score

To submit your video clip containing your response, please follow the guidelines below:

1. Record your video clip with audio using your smartphone or any device that outputs in a video format (.mov, .mp4, .avi etc).

2. Ensure that the video clip you have recorded does not exceed 6 minutes. **Any additional time exceeding 6 minutes will not be scored.**

3. Ensure that your face is visible and that your voice is audible in your clip. Your video clip will be processed to ensure it meets facial recognition. Clips that fail facial recognition will not be scored.

4. Once you are satisfied with your recording, visit https://apetest.com/edu/product/baseline and enter your redemption code at checkout to receive your free upload access code. Your redemption code can be found at the back of your book for purchases made from APE Advisor Prep. ***If you purchased your book from another retailer, you will need to pay the small nominal fee at checkout to use this service.**

5. After checkout, click on the link provided and enter your access code to upload your video clip.

6. Your APE Advisor Prep® MMI® Score will be available for download from MY APE portal and will provide valuable insight into where you stand relative to other applicants starting their MMInterview testing preparation.

12: Role Playing & Acting Scenarios

You are a medical student. Mr. Reed is a 52 year old male whom you saw four weeks ago in your outpatient clinic with your team. It has been two weeks since he underwent a prostate biopsy. Unfortunately the results of his prostate biopsy confirm a cancer diagnosis. He is here to find out the results of his biopsy. Upon arrival Mr. Reed is placed in an examining room by the nurse who subsequently informs you that he appears very anxious. Your preceptor would like you to go in and see Mr. Reed first and disclose the results of his biopsy.

Please enter the examining room and interact with Mr. Reed. During your encounter please discuss the results of his biopsy with him.

Scenario Discussion

As you start to mentally plan your upcoming encounter with Mr. Reed, remember that the interviewer in the room is not going to evaluate your knowledge of any aspects surrounding "prostate" cancer. However, making incorrect statements about prostate cancer treatment decisions or providing "advice" on prostate cancer will work against you and take away from your main goal of effectively delivering bad news.

General Approach to Acting & Role Playing Stations

Interviewees frequently cite role playing stations as being one of the most challenging categories because of their artificial settings and their unpredictable paths. You can't change the settings of these stations but with a few tricks we'll go over, we'll show you how to take control of these scenarios and keep the ball in your court.

Contrary to popular belief, the most important aspect of this role playing scenario is not to deliver the bad news regarding the results of Mr. Reed's prostate biopsy.   When faced with a role playing scenario such as this one, it is crucial to first determine the situational context displayed by the actor and to identify background cues. **Rushing in to deliver bad news prematurely often proves to be a very costly mistake in these stations.**

What is bad news?

Quite simply, bad news may be defined as "any information which adversely and seriously affects an individual's view of his or her future" [1]. Delivering bad news is complex and in addition to the verbal component of disclosing bad news, it also includes responding to the patient's emotional reactions, involving the patient in decision-making, dealing with the stress created by the patient's expectations for cure, the involvement of multiple family members, and the dilemma of how to give hope when the situation is bleak [2].

Why is delivering bad news important?

How bad news is disseminated to patients' will affect their level of comprehension, their level of hopefulness, subsequent psychological adjustment and ultimately their satisfaction with medical care received [3].   The effects of bad news on an individual's well-being are life changing. The process is stressful for both the provider and recipient.   Research suggests that physicians who are comfortable in delivering bad news may be subject to less stress and burnout [4].   If you already have an approach to delivering bad news, follow along and see how yours compares.

Start by taking a thorough look around at your environment. Make a mental note of the room setting (ie. quiet, noisy, private) and assess for accessories in the room (ie. tissue box, table, chair arrangements). *Ask yourself if the setting is appropriate for delivering bad news?*

It is important to have clear comprehension of what the individual already understands and the breadth of information they would like to know before diving in with any bad news.   A simple question to tease this information out is to ask, *"Are you the type of person that wants to know all the little details or do you prefer to have the big picture?*

If they are unaccompanied, make sure to address whether there is anyone else they'd like to have present for the discussion. Remember to pause after delivering bad news. Acknowledge emotions shown and let the individual know that "we will continue when they are ready". Be sure to have a clear understanding in your mind of what they need at this point prior to ending your discussion and the station.

Pocket 1: *What general category type of scenario is this MMInterview station?*

Answer: Role Play/Acting.

Pocket 2: *What is the main problem or issue in this MMInterview station?*

Answer: Considerations around delivering bad news and effective demonstration of empathy.

Pocket 3: *What is the main source of the problem or issue in this MMInterview station?*

Answer: Cancer is life changing and as humans, any big change is emotionally stressful.

Pocket 4: *What personal experience (if applicable) can I share in my response in this MMInterview station?*

Answer: It is generally not applicable to directly share your personal experience in role playing scenarios as this may negatively shift the emphasis away from the actor to you and detract from your ability to explore and provide empathy to the actor.

Pocket 5: *How would I resolve the problem or issue, taking into account my perspective and other perspectives for this MMInterview station?*

Answer: In the majority of role playing/acting stations, effective resolution requires you to take into account the actor's perspective and demonstrate your ability to be responsive and support their needs.

Sample Model Response

Applicant: *Enters room after knocking, greets Mr. Reed by shaking his hand and introduces themselves properly. "Hello Mr. Reed. Welcome back. Thank you for coming in today."*

Mr. Reed: "Thank you."

Applicant: "Mr. Reed. Do you remember why we did that biopsy on your prostate several weeks ago?"

Mr. Reed: "Well, we decided a biopsy was necessary to help understand why I am having trouble going to the bathroom."

Applicant: "We were hoping the biopsy would give us a better understanding of why you might be having difficulty going to the bathroom and it has. However before we talk about that in more detail, how have you been since your biopsy?"

Mr. Reed: "Unfortunately, very anxious."

Applicant: "You do look anxious. Is it because of the biopsy or because of something else?"

Mr. Reed: "Not knowing the results of the biopsy and fearing that I might have cancer are the reasons."

Applicant: "I understand. You mentioned cancer. Can you remind me whether you know anyone with cancer?

Mr. Reed: "Yes, but they have all passed."

Applicant: "I'm sorry to hear that Mr. Reed. I know it must be difficult for you to talk about this. I want to focus a bit more on you now that I understand that you've lost loved ones to cancer. Generally speaking, are you the type of person who likes to know all the details or do you prefer the big picture?"

Mr. Reed: "Big picture."

Applicant: "That's helpful for me to know. Did you come here by yourself today?"

Mr. Reed: "My brother is in the waiting room."

Applicant: *"Would you like me to bring him in for our discussion or is there anyone else you'd like to have present?"*

Mr. Reed: "That's ok. Thanks for asking."

Applicant: *"Mr. Reed, I know you're anxious because the thought of having "cancer" is there. Unfortunately, we do see cancer cells in your biopsy done a few weeks ago. (Pause)*

Mr. Reed: "So I have cancer?" (Starts to become emotional)

Applicant: *(Hands tissue box to patient) "I know this is life changing information but the biopsy results do show cancel cells in the prostate, Mr. Reed."*

Mr. Reed: "I'm sorry, I don't usually cry. Am I going to die?"

Applicant: *"I know a lot must be going through your mind right now. Before we talk about anything else, can you please tell me what you need from me right now?*

Mr. Reed: "I don't know. Can we talk about my treatment options for this cancer?"

Applicant: *"Mr. Reed, I can see how this is life changing information is affecting you. I want to make sure I have a better understanding of what I can do to support you first and foremost."*

Mr. Reed: "I'm not sure doc. I think I just need some time right now to let it all sink in."

Applicant: *"I understand. Would you like us to bring you back next week after you've had some time to let things sink in?*

Mr. Reed: "yes, thank you."

Applicant: *"If it's ok with you, I'm going to step out and update the rest of the team and I'll be back with them." (Shakes hand with Mr. Reed before leaving room)*

Avoid the Acting Station Pitfalls

This scenario would have likely been much more difficult and taken several turns for the worse if the applicant had fallen for Mr. Reed's traps by answering his questions on treatment options and whether he'll succumb from his cancer. Remember that you are not being evaluated on your knowledge base in a particular subject. In this case, it is impossible to make sound treatment recommendations based on the information given in the scenario.

Pitfall 1: **Avoid answering questions which require more information to assess.**

In this scenario, treatment and prognosis questions raised by the actor are meant to assess your ability to think on the spot. Providing false or inaccurate information about Mr. Reed's prognosis or treatment may actually hurt your score indirectly.

Pitfall 2: **Do not complete the task until you have a thorough understanding of the standardized actor's background and mentation.**

In this scenario, rushing in to deliver Mr. Reed's cancer diagnosis without first understanding his expectations, mental and emotional states would have likely lead to disaster. For acting stations, the key is to take your time to understand the person's contextual background first. Adopting this approach will save you a lot of time, stress and maximize your performance.

How to Steer Yourself Back On Track When Needed

However, let's assume that you had gone down the wrong path by talking about radiation therapy, chemotherapy or surgery as treatment options for Mr. Reed without knowing important prognostic factors for prostate cancer such as the PSA level or Gleason score. In such cases, it's important to have a get out of jail strategy in your back pocket. One key phrase that works well in most role playing scenarios is, *"Before I go into any more details about treatment options, can you please tell me what's going through your mind?"* If you get challenged and the individual insists that you continue down the same path regarding something you have no clue about, then just stand your ground and say, *"I hear what you are saying (Mr. Reed) and we will talk about your treatment but right now, I'm more worried about how this life changing information is affecting you. Is it ok if we spend a bit more time exploring this?"*

Remember, the MMInterviews are very much about showing you have control in your responses and being able to take on the heat (without sweating)!

References

1. Buckman R. Breaking Bad News: A Guide for Health Care Professionals. Baltimore: Johns Hopkins University Press, 1992:15.

2. Baile WF, et al. SPIKES—A Six-Step Protocol for Delivering Bad News: Application to the Patient with Cancer. The Oncologist 2000, 5:302-311

3. Butow PN, et al. Communication with cancer patients: does it matter? J Palliat Care 1995;11:34-38.

4. Ramirez AJ et al. Burnout and psychiatric disorder among cancer clinicians. Br J Cancer 1995;71:1263-1269

Station Notes

13: Traditional Themed Scenarios

Please discuss with the interviewer your decision to pursue a career as a physician.

In your answer, please include any relevant factor(s) that lead to your decision to apply to medical school.

Scenario Discussion

Most applicants are familiar with traditional interview type questions. However, due to time constraints placed on the interviewee by the MMInterview format, many applicants struggle to sufficiently manage their time during their initial response and subsequently during probing questions.

General Approach to Traditional Stations

Traditional themed MMInterview stations represent a true opportunity to share your unique story with the interviewer and should be embraced. These days, it's hard to practice medicine without hearing the term, "Evidence Based Medicine", a concept that also originates from McMaster University. Our founder, Dr. Kevyn To has worked with the father of EBM and in order to succeed on traditional themed MMInterview stations, you must be "critical" of your own experiences and incorporate this concept into your responses.

To do this, you'll need to organize and prioritize your personal experiences on paper first. We suggest maintaining a diary of your pertinent personal experiences highlighting relevant characteristics assessed. Most programs like to include an element of surprise to catch applicants off guard, by asking about "extreme" events that have occurred in their life. Be prepared and save yourself the panic on interview day.

We will go off on a slight tangent from our scenario to illustrate with an example involving conflict and failure to get you started.   Begin by brainstorming ideas in your mind around conflicts you've experienced and failures you've encountered in life.   Think about what happened, who it involved, what you've learned and what you'd do differently if faced with the same situation in the future.   Now jot down all your thoughts and organize them in a way that will make them easily accessible for you to refer back to in your mind on your actual interview day. As you write down your experiences, think about relevant buzz words that resonate to the applicable experience you are sharing. Using our example for conflict and failure, the appropriate "buzz" words could include, resiliency, communication and self-reflection. You don't need to hit every single buzz word but when a buzz word is used, it is important to provide evidence of the buzz word in action within your answer.

Let's discuss the hypothetical answer below:

"I experienced a conflict involving my research supervisor. We disagreed over how to allocate resources for my research project. I was ultimately able to solve this conflict through my excellent communication and collaboration skills."

What did you think about our hypothetical answer above?   If you felt that this is exactly the kind of answer you should avoid on your interview, then please give yourself a pat on the shoulder. The answer includes relevant buzz words but fails to justify and provide evidence showing how the applicant demonstrated excellent communication and collaboration skills.

Let's try again with another hypothetical answer.

"I experienced a conflict involving my research supervisor. I felt the research grant money should be used to purchase new equipment for our lab instead of hiring additional staff as my

supervisor suggested. I recognize the importance of open communication and highlighted several benefits of having new equipment that my supervisor had not considered and my supervisor did the same with respect to hiring additional staff. Together we were able to collaborate and compromise to benefit research and everyone in our lab."

Notice that in the second answer, we include "buzz" words to draw the evaluator's attention to our answer AND provide justification and evidence showing exactly how the buzz word qualities are demonstrated.

Getting back to the MMInterview station, a strong, credible answer to this station will allow the interviewer to clearly remember you from other interviewees. Your personal story if told correctly will make it obvious to the interviewer that you have placed significant emphasis and have undergone significant relevant experiences to adequately prepare yourself for a future career in medicine.

Why medicine and not another health profession?

Doctors interact daily with other health care professionals in multidisciplinary settings. The role of each health care professional is important in providing efficient, patient centered care. Physicians have largely shifted away from the captain of the ship model to a much more team based approach.

Therefore, it is just as important for you to be able to justify why other health care professions are not the best fit as it is for you to be able to confidently tell your interviewer why you want to go into medicine. To help you formulate your answer, please keep in mind the ways medicine differs from other health professions and ask yourself how are these differences able to better account for my fit in a career?

General approach to "Why Medicine?"

Even though "why medicine" is a highly personalized answer, a few general comments can be said about the components of a "strong" answer.

> ➢ A strong answer clearly identifies that the applicant has thought about other health care professions and has ultimately arrived at the conclusion that being a physician is the career that best suits them.

> ➢ A strong answer clearly shows that the applicant understands what the profession of medicine has to offer them and forms a strong evidence based bridge with their past experiences.

> ➢ A strong answer clearly portrays the applicant's interest in being a physician chronologically in such a way that shows adequate preparation for a career in medicine.

Avoid This Traditional Themed MMInterview Pitfall

Pitfall 3: **Do not fall into the trap of sounding rehearsed**

Rather than memorize entire preformed responses, focus on the main points you'd like to articulate in your answer. Memorize these highlights instead of paragraphs and your response and delivery will appear much more natural to the interviewer.

Sample Model Response

Interviewer: "Can you please tell me about your decision to pursue a career as a doctor."

Applicant: "My decision to apply to medical school to become a doctor is the result of all of my experiences. After learning about diseases in my undergraduate biology course, I began to think about health care as a career option and I wanted to explore this further. Over the years, I've sought out experiences in different health professions and enjoyed them to a certain degree but the field that is most satisfying and the best fit for me is medicine. However, being able to help people is not enough for me. I want a career that will allow me the flexibility to take care of people, be an educator and also conduct research. In terms of taking care of people, I really value the unique patient-doctor relationship I've observed in my volunteer work. I've also participated in medical research in my undergrad and this non-clinical aspect of medicine was very rewarding for me. These are just a few of the experiences I've sought out which have helped further solidify my decision to apply to medical school and become a physician."

Probing Questions

✓ What will you do if you don't get into medical school this year?

✓ What do you think is the most challenging aspect to being a physician?

✓ What do you think is the most rewarding aspect to being a physician?

✓ What do you think is the least rewarding aspect to being a physician?

Station Notes

Your dental school employs a peer assessment program that requires all 8 of your tutorial group classmates in your year to evaluate your performance in key areas on a numerical scale from 1 (low) to 10 (high). At the end of your first year of dental school, you receive the following evaluation below:

Shows appropriate empathy towards patients:

7.4 (class avg = 7.8)

Encourages communication and collaboration:

8.2 (class avg = 8.2)

Acknowledges one's own limitations and skills:

6.9 (class avg = 7.9)

Discuss with the interviewer how you feel about these results and what your next steps would be.

Scenario Discussion

Evaluations constitute an important forward component for any learner. They are available in all different shapes and sizes. Some are knowledge based and others like this example are peer based. In this scenario, you have scored below the class average in the key areas of "empathy" and "acknowledging your own limitations". These areas are difficult to objectively assess at any educational level due to their subjective nature and the lack of validated guidelines.

Empathy Basics

Empathy is a fundamental concept that plays an important role in facilitating quality health care. It is defined as a person's ability to accurately sense the patient's private world as if it were their own, but without ever losing the "as if" quality. *The four key domains of empathy include cognitive, emotive, moral and behavioral* [1]:

✓ The **cognitive** domain refers to a person's ability to identify and understand others' perspectives and predict their thoughts.

✓ The **emotive** domain describes the ability to experience and share in others' psychological states.

✓ The **moral** domain refers to an internal altruistic drive that motivates the practice of empathy.

✓ The **behavioral** dimension refers to the ability to communicate empathetic understanding and concerns.

The take home message for the purpose of the MMInterviews is that despite knowing a lot about the components of empathy, we do not have a good reliable tool to measure empathy [2]. Therefore to improve your score in the area of empathy, it is critical to focus on improvement within individual   components of empathy.

Acknowledging Your Own Limitations

It may not be obvious when you first read the prompt that this is really a weakness question bundled into a MMInterview format.

Acknowledging your own limitations is synonymous with being able to identify areas of weaknesses. However, recognizing your limitations isn't about signaling weakness or about admitting defeat. It's about empowering yourself to be more successful in your future endeavors.

When picking a weakness, the key is to pick a weakness that you have been able to make progress on. Be prepared and have at least two weaknesses ready to discuss. In the case of the MMInterviews, do not volunteer any personal weaknesses unless explicitly asked. Instead use "fictional" weaknesses that are relevant to the station. You may want to use a personal experience where you were able to help others overcome their weaknesses but the key is to not reveal your own weaknesses unless explicitly asked. Remember to put your best foot forward at all times.

Sample Model Response

Interviewer: "Can you please tell me how you feel about these evaluation results and discuss your next steps."

Applicant: "It's the end of my first year of dental school and I've just received peer evaluation scores in the domains of empathy, communications, and identifying my own limitations. I'm at the class average for communications but below the class average in the areas of empathy and acknowledging my own limitations. I feel disappointed at these results but I'm optimistic that I will be able to move forward and improve my performance in these areas for future evaluations. I'm also very appreciative of the feedback received from my peers in these domains. To improve my performance in the area of empathy, I would actively seek out feedback directly from my patients and my group members. In order to more effectively recognize my own limitations, I would first examine my own weaknesses in more detail and then seek out help from others to improve my performance in these areas. In terms of communications, I also want to see my performance improve further. I will reassess my own strengths, focus on non-verbal aspects of communication and increase my awareness of personal interactions. After taking all these measures, I would ask to receive evaluations at regular intervals to be able to better gauge my progress instead of waiting until the end of the academic year."

Probing Questions

- ✓ What does empathy mean to you?
- ✓ How would you monitor your results to ensure you are making progress?
- ✓ Are there any other individuals you would want to seek the help of?
- ✓ Where does time management fit into your action plan?

References

1. Morse JM. et al. Exploring empathy: a conceptual fit for nursing practice? Journal of Nursing Scholarship. 1992: 24(4), 273–280

2. Yu J. et al. Evaluation of empathy measurement tools in nursing: systematic review. Journal of Advanced Nursing. 2009 65(9), 1790–1806.

Station Notes

Each week you gather with your tutorial group to review material assigned to each team member from the previous week. The work is divided up among your group equally such that each team member is responsible for learning a specific aspect of the material and then reporting back to the rest of the group. You consistently feel frustrated with one member of the group who repeatedly comes to the group sessions late and unprepared.

Please discuss with the interviewer what you would do in this situation and be prepared to justify your response.

Scenario Discussion

This MMInterview station touches upon several themes including conflict management, group work and self-reflection. Interviewees frequently have little difficulty identifying the underlying conflict and group work themes of the scenario. However, self- reflection is also central to the scenario and is more often missed by interviewees.

What is Self-Reflection?

Self-reflection is the active conscious process of placing emphasis and thought into one's character, actions and motives. Combining self-reflection with structured learning is a useful tool for helping students increase self-awareness and ease anxiety that may interfere with learning [1].

General Approach to Traditional Group Work Stations

Before we can address any potential group dynamics that exist among the team, the interviewee has to first rule out any potential personal sources of bias that may exist. If there are potential biases, make sure to acknowledge and address those first.

Disagreements inevitably arise among group work. To remain cohesive as one unit, any potential concerns should first be brought up to the remaining group members minus the individual(s) with whom concerns have been identified. We have all heard casual statements from individuals claiming that "for any MMInterview station there is no such thing as a wrong answer." From my experience, having been in involved on both sides of the admissions' process, there are clearly wrong answers for EVERY MMInterview station. An incorrect approach in this situation would be to directly confront this team member immediately about their tardiness and lack of preparedness without first speaking to the other group members.

After first speaking with the group and establishing group consensus, the next step should be to identify how to bring up the issue(s) with the individual of concern. During the discussion, make sure to address both your concerns, the group's concerns and any personal concerns raised by the individual of concern. At this point offer them support when appropriate. Using pocket 3, we identify the perceived lack of cooperation among this team member as being the source of the problem (arriving late and being unprepared were two sources of frustration mentioned in the prompt). In your mind, explore possible reasons to account for this individual arriving late and unprepared.

Most of us have been in a situation involving a group conflict at some point so use these scenarios as opportunities for you to share your own personal experience with your interviewer. As you come up with your answer about what you would do in this situation, in the back of your mind, be prepared to justify why.

Avoid These Pitfalls during Your MMInterview

As you carefully read the MMInterview station prompt, you may have not paid any attention to the wording and gender descriptors. Notice that in this MMInterview scenario, the sex of the team member in question is not revealed. This is done deliberately in an attempt to catch you off guard and have you put your foot in your mouth.

Pitfall 4: **Avoid preconceived notions associated with gender and gender roles.**

Many applicants during mock MMInterview testing sessions tend to associate behaviors such as lack of cooperation with male gender and roles such as nursing with female gender. It's amazing how many times we've heard applicants assume the group member in this scenario is "male" and referred to them as "him" in their answer. Remember to be as gender neutral as the prompt you're reading.

Pitfall 5: **Remember the context of the scenario and do not overstep your boundaries**

In this situation, it may be easy to overlook the fact that you are working in a group and directly confront this individual without first seeking group input. Your approach to group work situations should be to resolve issues as a cohesive functional unit rather than as an overly confident and aggressive team member.

Sample Model Response

Interviewer: "Can you please tell me what you would do in this situation?"

Applicant: "This is a scenario where I'm a member of a weekly tutorial group and one of my classmates repeatedly comes to the sessions late and unprepared. I would first take a step back and ask myself if I might have any personal bias towards this group member that could be contributing to my feelings of frustration. Afterwards, I would meet with my group (without this individual present) and see if other members had any concerns about this individual before sharing mine. Assuming we are all on the same page, I would offer suggestions on how to proceed and ask for group feedback. I was involved in a similar group work situation in my undergrad history course and we were able to move forward by exploring the potential reasons why our team member was unprepared and late for our sessions. Once I knew the reasons, I was able to offer support to help them. Having been through a similar experience, I wouldn't want to confront this individual on my own without first undergoing self- reflection and making sure I had the support of my group."

Probing Questions

- ✓ Why should the other group members accept your suggestions?

- ✓ What will you do if things continue to persist with this same individual?

- ✓ What are some potential consequences of directly confronting this individual?

- ✓ Is there any role for reporting this individual's behavior to higher authority?

- ✓ Do you prefer to learn in groups or on your own?

References

1. Ganzer CA, et al. Structured learning and self-reflection: strategies to decrease anxiety in the psychiatric mental health clinical nursing experience. Nurs Educ Perspect. 2013 Jul-Aug;34(4):244-7.

Station Notes

14: Collaboration Scenarios

> Without using your hands, please *explain* to the interviewer how to tie shoelaces.

Scenario Discussion

Your initial reaction to this prompt was probably somewhere along the lines of "are you kidding me?" followed by "how the heck am I going to explain this to the interviewer?" During your initial pass through of the prompt, it may have also slipped your mind that this is a collaboration station. Many applicants have grown accustomed to the association that a collaboration station requires another "co-applicant". **This is no longer the case with the changing landscape of the MMInterview.** Any station involving you and another individual may in fact be a collaboration based station.

General Approach to Collaboration Stations

In this scenario the prompt provides the following clues to identify this station as being collaboration, task based. Many collaboration stations are visual based (such as tying shoelaces) in nature. The instructions also explicitly ask the applicant to "explain" to the interviewer. Verbs such as explain and interact often imply a collaboration station at hand.

For all collaboration stations, you should expect one or a combination of the following:

❖ **Delivering instructions to another person.**

❖ **Receiving instructions from another person.**

In this scenario, explaining to the interviewer how to tie shoelaces is synonymous with delivering instructions to them on how to achieve this.

When your role is to deliver instructions, it is important to complete the following at the beginning of your station:

- ❖ **Establish a supportive** framework with your co-applicant or third party. This can be done by introducing yourself and acknowledging that you are looking forward to working with them on this station.

- ❖ **Establish positive rapport** within your role with your co-applicant or third party, by letting them know this is a team effort and they should feel free to interrupt at any point if they have any difficulty understanding your instructions.

- ❖ **Establishing a sense of team based dynamics** by asking your co-applicant or third party, if it's ok to begin. Ensure you have a clear understanding of what information has been given to the other party and make sure you're both on the same page.

When your role is to receive instructions, adopt a more passive lens and complete the following throughout your station:

- ❖ **Establish a supportive** framework with your co-applicant or third party. This can be done by introducing yourself and acknowledging that you are looking forward to working with them on this station.

- ❖ **Demonstrate active listening** within your role by using positive fillers such as "I'm with you", "I understand" and "I'm ready to continue when you are". Do not interrupt your co-applicant or third party while they are speaking.

During your encounter, remember that it's **quality over quantity**. Do not rush and let your perceptions of the task or your partner's inability to receive instructions affect your mentation.

Many collaboration stations involve visual elements such as shapes, objects and drawings. To help you maximize your chances of success, keep in mind the following pearls of wisdom in order of importance.

1. If your station involves a drawing, always start with instructions for the simplest and most common elements first.

2. Think back to your audience and adjust your vocabulary as necessary to maximize comprehension. For instance, younger audiences tend to be more responsive to simple shapes and common animals. Use this difference to your advantage.

3. Be concise. Instead of describing objects independently, use linkage by associating current objects with missing elements.

4. Use colors to your advantage to show contrast, break down complex collaboration stations into more visual and manageable tasks for you and your partner.

Towards the end of your collaboration station, you and you partner may be required to provide feedback on each other's individual performance and performance as a team. Remember to keep it positive and only volunteer suggestions for improvement when explicitly prompted.

Sample Model Response

Interviewer: "Shall we get started?"

Applicant: "Sure thing! It's nice to meet you. My name is _____ and I'm looking forward to working with you."

Applicant: "It looks like I will be explaining to you how to tie shoelaces. Before I begin, please feel free to interrupt at any time. Also, if what I'm saying doesn't make sense, please let me know so that I can clarify or explain things differently."

Interviewer: "Thank you."

Applicant: "In this case, I'm not going to use my hands. Let's start by picturing a red colored shoelace in your right hand and a black colored shoelace in your left hand."

Applicant: "Are you still with me?"

Interviewer: "Yes, very much so."

Applicant: "Great! What we'll do now is cross the red lace over the black lace so that we have an X. Then we're going to pull the red lace which is on top through the bottom of this X with our right index finger/thumb and bring it towards you. Now, picture holding the ends of each lace into a bunny ear. You're going to cross the black bunny ear over the red bunny ear."

Applicant: "Please let me know if you have any questions so far?"

Interviewer: "So far so good."

Applicant: "We're coming up to the most difficult part now, so I'm going to take my time. By now there should be a hole between the bunny ears. Picture the bunny running around this hole with its ears flopping. Then the bunny suddenly sees a dog and jumps into the hole, with his red ear going through first. Unfortunately the dog was able to grab the bunny's black ear. At this point, the bunny's ears are being pulled in opposite directions and ultimately form a solid knot."

Applicant: "Please let me know if you need me to repeat anything I've said?"

Interviewer: "I was able to follow along with your story. That's a very effective way to explain how to tie shoelaces."

Applicant: "Thank you for allowing me the opportunity."

Station Notes

15: Ethical, Social & Policy Scenarios

The belief held by many Aboriginals is that they come from the land. This plays a great deal of importance in discussing ceremonies about death. You are a funeral home manager looking after funeral arrangements for Mr. Acorn; a 55 year old Aboriginal who passed unexpectedly from a heart attack two days ago. He has not left behind any advanced directives. His wife of 33 years strongly believes he should be buried whereas his parents strongly oppose a burial and believe he should be cremated with his ashes scattered over the land. You cannot proceed any further with Mr. Acorn's funeral arrangements until a decision is made regarding the type of burial.

Please discuss with the interviewer how you would handle this situation.

Scenario Discussion

Over the last 3 years, the emphasis on pure bioethics within the MMInterviews has decreased. *Applicants are not required to have any expert knowledge in ethics but should be comfortable with recognizing and discussing the guiding principles in healthcare of beneficence, non-maleficence, autonomy and informed consent.*

General Approach to Ethical Based Scenarios

Ethical stations on the MMInterview often involve a dilemma or conflict and are often very easy to identify. The challenge with ethical stations often lies in the complexity of the issues raised and the time limits imposed by the interview station.

This MMInterview station highlights real world challenges that can happen when a loved one dies unexpectedly without having established a clear set of advanced directives. The situation is further complicated by Mr. Acorn's parents' cultural background which holds a different belief system than that of Mr. Acorn's wife. In coming up with your own answer to this scenario, please remember that our ultimate goal in this case is to use ethical principles to make the best possible decision by carrying out Mr. Acorn's final wishes.

The basis of Aboriginal beliefs

Aboriginal beliefs are rooted in the context of oral history and culture. For Aboriginal people, autonomy and decision-making is best understood as a process and not as the correct interpretation of a unified code [1]. Mr. Acorn's parents were likely raised in a belief system that emphasizes achieving balance and wellness within the domains of human life (mental, physical, emotional and spiritual). They believe that spreading his ashes over the land likely represents this balance symbolically and minimizes harm to their culture and Mr. Acorn's spiritual future.

Substitute Decision Making

On the other hand, Mr. Acorn's wife of 33 years seems to believe that her husband should be buried. In any situation where the patient is not able to advocate for themselves, a substitute decision maker should be carefully selected. The substitute decision-maker should be the person or persons with the best knowledge of the patient's specific wishes, the patient's values and beliefs and should have the patient's best interests at heart [2]. Keep in mind the difference between values, beliefs and wishes. The patient's wishes are those preferences expressed by the patient that are relevant to the decision that needs to be made.

Values and beliefs are generally less specific than wishes but allow the substitute decision-maker to infer, in light of other choices the patient has made (ie. their approach to life), what they would decide in the present situation. When family members disagree on which course of action to take, they should be encouraged to focus their attention towards what the patient would have wanted.

The criteria on which the decision should be based on are [2]:

1. **The patient's previously explicitly stated wishes.**
2. **The patient's known values and beliefs.**
3. **The patient's best interests.**

The Provider's Role in Substitute Decision Making

Simply stated, the health care professional's role here is to facilitate the process of substitute decision-making by providing information that will result in an informed choice on the patient's behalf, while doing no harm to the patient's wishes and balancing the dialogue between his family. Health care professionals act as chaperones in the process and help guide the substitute(s) to consider the patient's previously expressed wishes, their values and beliefs, and their best interests [2].

Pocket 1: *What general category type of scenario is this MMInterview station?*

Answer: Ethical with elements of Cultural Competency.

Pocket 2: *What is the main problem or issue in this MMInterview station?*

Answer: Conflict between the patient's spouse and family belief systems requiring ethical guidance.

Pocket 3: *What is the main source of the problem or issue in this MMInterview station?*

Answer: Lack of written advance directives provided by the patient.

Pocket 4: *What personal experience (if applicable) can I share in my response in this MMInterview station?*

Answer: Brainstorm for experiences in which you were able to successfully act as a mediator and facilitate a resolution among conflicted individuals. The experience you share does not have to be health care related.

> **Pocket 5:** *How would I resolve the problem or issue, taking into account my perspective and other perspectives for this MMInterview station?*
>
> Answer: In the majority of ethical stations, effective resolution requires you to share your perspective of the valid principles and attempt to reconcile them with conflicting perspectives. In this scenario, the goal is to use ethical principles to make the best possible decision by carrying out Mr. Acorn's final wishes.

Sample Model Response

Interviewer: "Can you please tell me how you would handle this situation?"

Applicant: "As the funeral home manager, this is a scenario where there is disagreement between family members regarding the proper end of life burial procedures. Mr. Acorn's autonomy is at risk here because he has not left behind any advanced directives and while his wife believes that her husband should be buried, Mr. Acorn's parents believe that their son should be cremated. Unfortunately, this illustrates the complexities that arise when no previous substitute decision maker or advanced directives are in place. I would have a thorough discussion individually with both his wife and his parents about Mr. Acorn's belief system. I would also speak with anyone else that may have played a significant part in his life such as close friends or children. As I speak to these individuals, I would consider the ethical principle of doing no harm to Mr. Acorn's wishes while balancing this between his family members. I would also try to maximize Mr. Acorn's autonomy. After having gathered these pieces of the puzzle, I would share my findings with his parents and his wife in the hopes of coming to a mutual agreement on how to proceed in the best interests of Mr. Acorn."

Probing Questions

✓   What would you do next if there was still no agreement on Mr. Acorn's burial procedures?

✓   What values and beliefs are most important in guiding your decision in this scenario?

✓   Who do you ultimately feel should have the final say in this scenario?

✓   Are there other individuals you would enlist the help of?

References

1. Ellerby JH, et al. Bioethics for clinicians: 18. Aboriginal cultures. CMAJ October 3, 2000 vol. 163 no. 7.

2. Lazar NM, et al. Bioethics for clinicians: 5: Substitute Decision Making. CMAJ 1996; 155: 1435-1437

Station Notes

The current average outpatient wait time in your area for an MRI scan is 120 days. This extended waiting period has sparked a growing concern from the general public who deems this wait time to be unacceptable. You are hired as a consultant to examine the current situation and make recommendations.

Please discuss your recommendation(s) with the interviewer.

Scenario Discussion

After reading the prompt, did the thought cross your mind that you're dealing with a scenario whereby increased wait times to MRIs could cause harm to patients? In this station, you're not asked to state the ethical principles but we'll be using them to guide our recommendations. Before we go further, let's briefly explore the importance of resource allocation.

What is resource allocation?

Resource allocation is the distribution of goods and services to programs and people. In the context of healthcare, macroallocations of resources are made by governments at the national, provincial / state and municipal levels [1]. Mesoallocations are made at the level of institutions and microallocations are made at the level of the individual patient [1].

Why is resource allocation important?

As public and professional expectations continue to increase, costly new technologies must be balanced against tightly monitored health care budgets, competing government priorities and provincial deficits [1]. In this scenario, a of lack of resources would include inadequate number of MRI machines, inadequate facilities to house MRI machines and/or inadequate number of properly trained personnel to operate MRI machines. Examples of resource allocation considerations would include parameters around how the MRI machines are used such as number of hours or days per week the machines are operated, the number of MRI scans being ordered by each provider, and the cost of educating the public and health force on proper utilization of MRI scans.

At this point, you should formulate an opinion for each of the above examples and possible solutions to the above considerations. As you come up with your recommendations, in the back of your mind, be prepared to defend why your recommendations should be accepted.

Pocket 1: *What general category type of scenario is this MMInterview station?*

Answer: Ethical with elements of Health Policy.

Pocket 2: *What is the main problem or issue in this MMInterview station?*

Answer: Increased wait times are unacceptable to the general public and may cause harm to patients/society.

Pocket 3: *What is the main source of the problem or issue in this MMInterview station?*

Answer: Lack of resources or inadequate resource allocation.

Pocket 4: *What personal experience (if applicable) can I share in my response in this MMInterview station?*

Answer: Brainstorm for personal experiences in which you were able to successfully balance the priorities of multiple groups or individuals. In this station, experiences that highlight your ability to act as an advocate and manage priorities are most relevant.

Pocket 5: *How would I resolve the problem or issue, taking into account my perspective and other perspectives for this MMInterview station?*

Answer: Explore the challenges associated with lack of resources and resource allocation. In your answer, refer to ethical principles to guide you towards making your recommendations.

Sample Model Response

Interviewer: "Please discuss your recommendations for this scenario."

Applicant: "This is a scenario where the public has grown concerned about the lengthy wait times to obtain an outpatient MRI scan. I recognize that this is a complex situation. As always, one of my main goals is to minimize harm to patients while maximizing accessibility and fairness for all patients. I would carefully explore the issues of resource allocation and lack of resources. After doing so, my recommendations would be to implement a provider tracking system to better understand how MRI appointments are being filled by physicians and to make changes to the way the MRI machines might currently be operated. In helping me arrive at my recommendations, I've found that the lengthy wait times were partly contributed by factors such as reduced MRI machine operating hours, as well as MRI scans being ordered for inpatients when they weren't indicated which further lengthened the wait times for outpatient MRI scans."

Probing Questions

- ✓ What other factors have you consider in making your recommendations?

- ✓ What will you do if the wait times don't improve 1 year after your recommendations are adopted?

- ✓ Where do you see the role of patient education fitting into this scenario?

- ✓ Is there anything else you'd like to mention that has not yet been covered?

References

1. McKneally MF, et al. Bioethics for clinicians: 13. Resource allocation. Can Med Assoc J 1997;157:163-7

Station Notes

You are a family physician with a busy clinic. Your next patient is Mr. Diode, an elderly gentleman who has been under your care for his type II diabetes, asthma and recurring angina. He was last seen by you 5 weeks ago. You quickly review his chart prior to seeing him today, and to your disappointment, you realize that his last electrocardiogram tracing done 6 weeks ago shows an abnormal ST segment elevation. The report was received in your office before Mr. Diode's last visit but you have not seen these results until now.

Please discuss what you would say to Mr. Diode with the interviewer.

Scenario Discussion

The first thing you've probably noticed is that the vocabulary used in this MMInterview scenario is more technical than other examples we've seen. The scenario is filled with medical jargon such as "angina" and "ST segment elevation" which would throw many medical school applicants off. Fortunately, this type of MMInterview station is likely to appear on a postgraduate residency interview (but in theory could appear on any health MMInterview circuit). There is no denying that it would be helpful to understand that angina means chest pain and to know that the significance of ST segment elevation on an electrocardiogram is that the heart is not receiving enough oxygen to meet its demands.

However, the above medical knowledge is not a prerequisite for performing well on this station as we'll continue to demonstrate using our APE KISS IT approach. There is more than enough information provided in laymen's terms in the prompt to allow any applicant to effectively succeed.

The primary objective in this station is honesty and whether an applicant is able to be responsible and accountable for mistakes they may make. **Honesty** is consistently reported as one of the most important personal attributes of physicians within the medical education literature and may be the attribute that instills trust at all levels of medical practice [1]. This MMInterview station falls under the ethical category (Pocket 1) and the main issue is omission of information (Pocket 2). The main source of the issue is that important medical information was not disclosed to the patient five weeks ago by their doctor (Pocket 3). Pocket 4 deals with any relevant personal experience you have to share regarding honesty and trust. Last but not least, Pocket 5 requires you to come up with your own response and you should do so after reading the scenario discussion but before reading the sample model response.

Stations with "Difficult Language Syndrome"

The MMInterviews are generally designed to be more stressful compared to the traditional personal interview due to their standardized nature. Given the tight time constraints, there is little to no emphasis on getting to know the applicant on a personal level. Rather, the MMInterviews aim to strategically expose your personal qualities and weaknesses through a standardized approach.

It is not uncommon to experience unfamiliar language in a MMInterview prompt. Difficult Language Syndrome (DLS) refers to the use of words that are unreasonably beyond the scope of the applicant's vocabulary. If you find yourself in such a situation, ask yourself what is the overall big picture in this prompt? Using our example, the overall big picture minus DLS is that as a physician, you've missed an important result when you saw this patient five weeks ago. You are seeing them now and have the opportunity to move forward with this new information.

Do not fall victim to those DLS distractors which in this case, will take you away from your ability to focus on the reasons why you may have missed this critical information five weeks ago and how you can prevent a recurrence.

Sample Model Response

Interviewer: "Can you please discuss what you would say to Mr. Diode in this situation?"

Applicant: "As Mr. Diode's physician, I'm seeing him for a 5 week follow up visit and after reviewing his chart I've noticed that he had an EKG test 6 weeks ago which shows an abnormality. However, this is my first time being aware of these results. I would begin by asking how he is doing and if there have been any changes since we last met. Assuming no changes have taken place since our last encounter, I would start a conversation regarding the missed EKG result. I would notify him that he had an EKG test done 6 weeks ago and the results were mailed to my attention shortly thereafter but I did not see them until today. After acknowledging and being honest about my mistake, I'll let him know that I'm in the process of setting up changes on how patient results are processed in the office in order to prevent this from happening again to anyone. I would offer any support he needs regarding my mistake. When we are both mutually satisfied with the discussion, I would shift gears and focus on Mr. Diode's current medical condition."

Probing Questions

- ✓ How would you explain to Mr. Diode exactly what has happened?

- ✓ What are some consequences of being honest in this situation?

- ✓ How would you respond if Mr. Diode became angry?

- ✓ Describe in detail how you can prevent a recurrence of this nature in the future?

References

1. Hofmeister M. et al. The Acceptability of the Multiple Mini Interview for Resident Selection. Residency Education Nov-Dec 2008 734.

Station Notes

You are a pharmacy student doing a clinical rotation on the surgical floor at a community hospital. It is early in the morning and after rounding, the surgical team members have departed for the operating room. You are about to go into a room to speak with Ms. Carol about her diabetes medication when her shift nurse pulls you aside and informs you she gave Ms. Carol 5 times the regular ordered dose of her blood pressure medication 20 minutes ago. The nurse has tried to page the surgery team twice but has been unsuccessful. No prescribed changes were made to Ms. Carol's medication record over the past 24 hours. You are the first person to be notified of this new information and the nurse tells you that Ms. Carol is currently stable and comfortable.

Please discuss the course of action you would take with the interviewer. In your answer, please explore the issues pertinent to this scenario.

Scenario Discussion

This MMInterview station highlights that errors are inevitable and real in the health care setting. Medical professionals will face situations where they must address mistakes that have been made with their patients. In most cases, errors are not the result of a single factor such as negligence but rather a complex array of interconnected factors. In this scenario, a medication error is reported to you and an ethical dilemma arises because the patient remains unaware that they were given five times the prescribed dose of their blood pressure medication.

What is a Medical Error?

Medical errors are usually considered to be preventable adverse medical events and are the result of omission or commission [1].

Important considerations for Medical Errors

The disclosure of a medical error represents a challenging ethical situation for health care providers [2]. Before full disclosure can occur, patient safety must take precedence.

Patient safety is of utmost importance after any committed medical error and must be fully addressed with the most responsible medical team. In more challenging scenarios where the medical error did not result in harm, it should automatically be assumed that the patient would want full disclosure, regardless of the magnitude of the medical error.

The full disclosure process should follow the guidelines for delivering bad news and take place in a private setting, when the patient is medically stable and is able to comprehend the discussion.

Lack of trust is a reality after a medical error has been disclosed. Patients often experience a loss of trust in the medical system and the involved health care team members when informed that a mistake has been made [3]. However, with an open dialogue, this loss of trust can be subsequently regained in comparison with the permanent loss of trust that results when a patient confirms that their health care team has not been fully transparent in their care.

As you formulate your answer to our scenario involving Ms. Carol, pay close attention to the main source of the issue/problem. In this case, a medical error has occurred but digging a little deeper below the surface, one could ask, why did the nurse give 5x the prescribed dose? Could the nurse have been a new employee and inexperienced? Perhaps this was her first time taking care of this patient and she misread the prescription order in Ms. Carol's chart?

Remember that when it comes to the MMInterviews, examining for the source of the issue/problem will not require any explicit clinical or subject based knowledge. Instead, use your common background knowledge and the information provided in the prompt to prioritize the important considerations we've illustrated. Ultimately ask yourself, how might this medical error have been prevented and approach it from both the nurse's and the patient's perspectives.

Pocket 1: *What general category type of scenario is this MMInterview station?*

Answer: Ethical.

Pocket 2: *What is the main problem or issue in this MMInterview station?*

Answer: Should full disclosure of this mistake and regard for patient safety override any consequences that might occur from this error.

Pocket 3: *What is the main source of the problem or issue in this MMInterview station?*

Answer: Medication error involving an overdose of prescribed therapy.

Pocket 4: *What personal experience (if applicable) can I share in my response in this MMInterview station?*

Answer: Brainstorm for personal experiences in which you faced a difficult situation but were ultimately able to make the "right" decision. In this station, experiences that highlight personal qualities such as honesty and professionalism are most relevant.

Pocket 5: *How would I resolve the problem or issue, taking into account my perspective and other perspectives for this MMInterview station?*

Answer: Explore the challenges associated with patient safety, full disclosure from multiple perspectives and convince the interviewer of your empathy towards this patient and how this error might have been prevented in the first place.

Sample Model Response

Interviewer: "Can you please discuss the course of action you would take in this situation?"

Applicant: "I'm the first to be notified by Ms. Carol's nurse that a medical error was made resulting in her receiving 5x the prescribed dose of her blood pressure medication. Even though Ms. Carol is currently stable and comfortable, the most pressing issue remains patient safety. She should be carefully monitored for any changes in discomfort or symptoms. I would next address this medical error with full disclosure to my supervisor, the surgical team and to Ms. Carol. By telling the patient that a mistake has been made, this would probably affect her outlook on the quality of care she has received. However, only by being fully honest and accountable do we stand the best chance of regaining her trust. To better understand why a mistake has been made, I would want to speak in more detail with her nurse regarding the exact surrounding circumstances in the hopes that similar errors could be prevented in the future."

Probing Questions

- ✓ What might you suggest to the nurse to help prevent similar future errors from happening?

- ✓ Is there a role for reporting the nurse to higher authority?

- ✓ Who should ultimately be held accountable for this medical error?

- ✓ Are there circumstances where it would be justified not to fully disclose that a medical error was made to the patient?

References

1. Brennan T. et al. Incidence of adverse events and negligence in hospitalized patients: results of the Harvard Medical Practice Study I. N Engl J Med 1991;324:370-6.

2. Hilfiker D. Facing our mistakes. N Engl J Med 1984;310:118-22.

3. Diekema DS. ETHICS IN MEDICINE University of Washington School of Medicine. Online. Accessed October 8, 2013

Station Notes

You are a senior medical student interested in becoming a pediatrician. It is the first day of your outpatient pediatrics elective. The staff pediatrician has asked you to tag along to see David, a 6 year old child brought in by his parents with a cough. Shortly after the encounter, the staff pediatrician tells you they feel sorry for David, as he has two dads. They believe that this is morally unacceptable because it will put David at increased risk for psychiatric disorders such as depression when he gets older. However, there is no scientific evidence to support the pediatrician's belief that children with same sex parents are at increased risk of psychiatric disorders. You feel something must be done about this situation.

Please discuss the course of action you would take with the interviewer.

Scenario Discussion

How many of you were thinking that this was a male pediatrician? If you answered yes, you're not alone! This is likely because from an early age, we are programmed to believe that women (as mothers) are more accepting and nurturing (and vice versa for men). However, keep in mind that the pediatrician's gender was never disclosed! Once again, remember not to fall for the gender assumption and gender roles pitfall!!

Both healthcare providers and patients may bring cultural, religious and ideological beliefs with them as they enter into a mutual patient-physician relationship. Occasionally, these beliefs may challenge or conflict with what the physician believes to be medically acceptable [1]. Medical encounters are generally a source of anxiety for the general population. For gay and lesbian patients, such normal stresses are further magnified by concerns related to sexual orientation [2]. In our MMInterview station, David's parents do not engage in a direct patient-physician relationship with the staff pediatrician but the physician's comments suggest that the patient-physician relationship with David may be negatively affected by their belief system and false perceptions of David's environment. In other words, we are dealing with provider bias.

What is Cultural Competency?

Cultural competency is the ability to interact effectively with people of different cultures and socio-economic backgrounds without bias. The concept of cultural competency has a positive effect on patient care delivery by enabling providers to deliver care that is respectful of and responsive to the health beliefs, practices and cultural and linguistic needs of diverse patients [3].

Important considerations for Cultural Competency

Developing cultural competency is critical to reducing health disparities and improving access to high-quality health care, health care that is respectful of and responsive to the needs of diverse patients [3].

Self-identification by the patient or individual group is a key consideration of cultural competency.   This involves using language and dialogue similar to that used by the individual to establish better understanding and rapport.

Advocating for patients is at the heart of cultural competency. In this scenario, David's parents are not aware of their pediatrician's belief system.   However, as a medical student working on the rotation, you are privy to this new information and to not advocate for David and his family would be acting like the "elephant in the room".

However, from your perspective as an aspiring pediatrician, confronting your pediatrician staff might be equivalent to committing career suicide and you may be labeled as a trouble maker for stirring the pot. One very important aspect you'll experience as a doctor is that it will be much more difficult to do the right thing at times, rather than to just turn a blind eye. However, at the end of the day, you're going to be the one that has to live with the consequences of your choices.

One approach for bringing up concerns with a superior is to start with the facts and ask for clarification. With David's case, you could ask for the evidence behind the pediatrician's comments. The main reasons for bringing up concerns with this pediatrician are to advocate for David, his family and improve the overall quality of healthcare. Your goal is not to complain about the past so we're not going to go there. You can use information from the past to inform the situation, but make sure to stay focused on what needs to be done to move forward so that patients are not subjected to provider bias.

Sample Model Response

Interviewer: "Can you please discuss the course of action you would take in this situation?"

Applicant: "This is the first day on my pediatrics elective and I've been told by my staff that the patient we just saw will have a higher chance of developing psychiatric conditions when he gets older because he has two dads. I would ask to speak with my staff in private, seek clarification and supporting evidence behind their comments. My main goal from our discussion is to improve the quality of care provided to David and future patients like David by not subjecting them to provider bias. However, by speaking with my staff, this may negatively affect my chances of become a pediatrician. I was in a similar situation at work where I interacted with my superior about management concerns and despite thinking that it was going to be job suicide, it ended up improving the dynamics of our work environment. Alternatively, by not speaking up, I would be the elephant in the room and for me, that isn't an option."

Probing Questions

✓ What are other relevant considerations for this scenario?

✓ Is it appropriate and/or necessary to disclose to David's parents the staff pediatrician's beliefs regarding same sex families?

✓ What are the challenges to achieving cultural competency?

✓ How does provider bias affect patient care?

References

1. Diekema DS. Cross-cultural Issues and Diverse Beliefs. Ethics in Medicine: University of Washington School of Medicine. Web. Accessed Oct 13th, 2013.

2. Stein GL, et al. Original Research: Physician–Patient Relationships among the Lesbian and Gay Community. Journal of the Gay   and   Lesbian   Medical Association September 2001, Volume 5, Issue 3, pp 87-93

3. NIH Communication: Cultural Competency
http://www.nih.gov/clearcommunication/cult uralcompetency.htm accessed Oct 13th, 2013

Station Notes

High-Yield Multiple Mini Interview Scenarios

(this page is intentionally left blank)

Tips To Remember ....

- Show up at least 35 minutes earlier than your scheduled time.

- <u>Always</u> ask the interviewer a question when prompted "do you have any questions?"

- Do not ramble on in your answer for more than <u>THREE</u> minutes at a time. Pause and assess for body language/cues.

- Read everything <u>carefully</u> and remember to always follow instructions!

- Do your background reading about the program, city and institution ahead of time.

- Show confidence in your answers but respect that everyone will have weak points, including yourself.

- For traditional interviews ask ahead of time for your interviewers' names and google them if possible.

- For MMInterviews, be familiar with the interview structure and logistics ahead of time.

- Don't read more into the question/scenario then there really is.

- Don't leave your interview preparation until the last minute.

- Go into the interview with the attitude that your hard work will pay off and that you will get into the program for which you are interviewing.

16: High-Yield Practice Scenarios

How to get the most out of your preparation

The following high yield MMInterview scenarios have been carefully selected to provide you with the most high-yield practice currently available. To get the most out of your interview preparation from this book, ensure that your responses are completed under the same simulated conditions as your actual interview.

Select sample model answers to the practice MMInterview scenarios have been included. The remaining answers may be discussed during your MMI® testing sessions for APE students.

If you are not an APE student and would like to learn more about how APE Advisor Prep® can help you with one-on-one MMInterview testing, please visit:

http://mminterview.com

-Station 01-

Multiple Mini Interview: 131203001

INSTRUCTIONS: You have **two** minutes to read the scenario below. You will have **eight** minutes to complete this station. Please do not enter the room until you are instructed to do so.

You are hired by the local zoo as an animal trainer to work with a new pair of chimpanzee monkeys. The zoo would like to set up an exhibit that allows the pair of chimpanzees to safely interact with the zoo visitors.   This requires that the chimpanzees be fully trained and responsive to commands. Upon meeting the pair of chimpanzees, you observe that they are very occupied and distracted. Despite offering treats, you are not able to get their full attention.

Please discuss with the interviewer your plan to succeed in training these two chimpanzees.

Sample Model Response

Interviewer: "Can you please discuss your plan to succeed?"

Applicant: "This is a scenario where I'm an animal trainer hired by the local zoo to work with a new pair of chimpanzees. The zoo wants the pair to be fully responsive by the end of the training period. Currently they seem distracted and preoccupied by their new environment and they're eager to explore their new surroundings. I would use their curiosity to my advantage and spend as much time as possible to closely observe their behaviors and their adjustment process to the new environment. In order for me to succeed, it will be crucial to be able to speak the same language as my chimpanzees.

This involves teaching them and helping them learn by association. I plan on doing this by rewarding positive behavior and clearly establishing a beginning and an end to our training sessions. I'm also aware that it is possible for my chimpanzees to learn unintentional behaviors from their surrounding so I would also be cautious to seek these out and minimize them. I would maximize the zoo's assistance from additional staff and trainers to help ensure we meet our goal. I have been involved in training a variety of animals in my past experiences and I successfully achieved my goals by adopting a similar plan."

Probing Questions

- ✓ What will you do if you do not meet your deadline to have the chimpanzees trained?

- ✓ Are there any other individuals you would seek the help of to achieve your goal?

- ✓ What are some potential consequences of not meeting your deadline to have the chimpanzees trained?

- ✓ What would you say to your supervisor if you had to ask them for an extension?

Sample Score Sheet

Please rate the applicant's overall performance on this station relative to all applicants you are rating. Do not assign a score more than once (ie. if assessing 10 applicants, you may only use a score of 10 once). You may adjust your scores before submitting.

Consider the applicant's:

     Ability to communicate effectively
     Strength of the arguments displayed
     Suitability for the program

Please place an "X" in the desired box below:

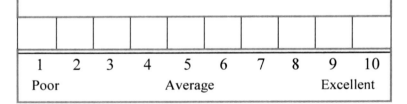

1	2	3	4	5	6	7	8	9	10
Poor				Average				Excellent	

Comments:

Station Notes

-Station 02-

Multiple Mini Interview: 160328011

INSTRUCTIONS: You have **two** minutes to read the scenario below. You will have **eight** minutes to complete this station. Please do not enter the room until you are instructed to do so.

As the transport minister, a new bill, HB-428 has been proposed that would make helmets optional for adult motorcyclists. The debates among proponents and opponents of this new bill, including the transport committee have been very heated with no end in sight. Insurance and motorcycle helmet producing companies are in strict opposition to this new bill moving any further in the legislation process and they have threatened to take all necessary means to ensure that it does not pass.

Please discuss with the interviewer how you would proceed in this situation.

Probing Questions

✓ Would you support bill HB-428?

✓ What would you do if the other members of the transportation committee did not support your course of action on bill HB-428?

✓ What issues are raised in this scenario?

✓ Is there anything else you'd like to discuss before we finish?

Sample Score Sheet

Please rate the applicant's overall performance on this station relative to all applicants you are rating. Do not assign a score more than once (ie. if assessing 10 applicants, you may only use a score of 10 once). You may adjust your scores before submitting.

Consider the applicant's:

       Ability to communicate effectively

       Strength of the arguments displayed

       Suitability for the program

Please place an "X" in the desired box below:

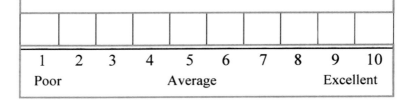

1	2	3	4	5	6	7	8	9	10
Poor				Average				Excellent	

Comments:

Station Notes

-Station 03-

INSTRUCTIONS: You have **two** minutes to read the scenario below. You will have **eight** minutes to complete this station. Please do not enter the room until you are instructed to do so.

You are a nutritionist working with a family doctor in your community. Along with the family doctor, you have formulated a care plan for a patient who was recently diagnosed with diabetes (type II). The patient is unaware that they have diabetes. Upon their return to see you, they feel great and ask for the results of their recent blood sugar testing.

Please discuss with the interviewer how you would proceed in this situation.

Sample Model Response

Interviewer: "Can you please discuss how you would proceed in this situation?"

Applicant: "This is a scenario where I'm a nutritionist working with a family doctor in my community. I'm about to see a patient in follow up who is unaware of their new diabetes diagnosis. It sounds like things are going well for them and at this point, they're inquiring about the results of their recent blood sugar testing. I would not rush to disclose their blood sugar results immediately. In this situation, it is really important for me as a team member to take a step back and assess their request. As a nutritionist, it would be inappropriate for me to disclose to the patient that they have diabetes based on their blood sugar results prior to them seeing their family physician first. As a team member, I would act in the most respectful way towards each person's role and boundaries. It's clear from the scenario that this patient has not yet been told they have diabetes by their doctor.

However, depending on my relationship with their family doctor and assuming that it was clearly communicated and acceptable for me to assist the family doctor by initiating a discussion surrounding this patient's new diabetes diagnosis, I would then proceed and disclose that their blood sugar results show a high level that fits with diabetes. At this point, I would offer my support and expertise in areas of lifestyle, nutrition and diet modification to help maximize their sugar control. I would ask when they're scheduled to see their physician and schedule a follow up appointment in my office after their physician appointment. In my experience as an ER volunteer, I've noticed that patient care is optimum when team boundaries are met with respect."

Probing Questions

- ✓ What are some relevant challenges to delivering bad news?

- ✓ In addition to the family physician, what other health care professionals are important in this patient's care?

- ✓ What will you do if the patient refuses to accept your care plan?

- ✓ Is it primarily the family doctor's responsibility to inform this patient of their diabetes diagnosis prior to seeing you?

Sample Score Sheet

Please rate the applicant's overall performance on this station relative to all applicants you are rating. Do not assign a score more than once (ie. if assessing 10 applicants, you may only use a score of 10 once). You may adjust your scores before submitting.

Consider the applicant's:

      Ability to communicate effectively

      Strength of the arguments displayed

      Suitability for the program

      Please place an "X" in the desired box below:

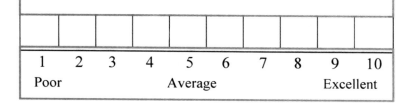

1	2	3	4	5	6	7	8	9	10
Poor				Average				Excellent	

Comments:

Station Notes

-Station 04-

Multiple Mini Interview: 1032020115

INSTRUCTIONS: You have **two** minutes to read the scenario below. You will have **eight** minutes to complete this station. Please do not enter the room until you are instructed to do so.

You are currently on your emergency medicine rotation. A 45 year old female struck by a vehicle while crossing the street has just arrived via ambulance and is in critical condition.   She is unconscious but breathing on her own and has experienced significant blood loss. The ER nurse gets ahold of her husband and he is told to come to the emergency department immediately. As he arrives, both the senior medical resident and staff physician are busy keeping the patient alive. There is a possibility that she may not survive and they have asked you to have a brief discussion with patient's husband to update him on his wife's current situation and to gather more information about what should be done should her heart stop beating. The ED nurse tells you that her husband is waiting in the family room. You head towards the family room to meet him.

Please interact with her husband. During your encounter, please clarify her end of life wishes.

Sample Score Sheet

Please rate the applicant's overall performance on this station relative to all applicants you are rating. Do not assign a score more than once (ie. if assessing 10 applicants, you may only use a score of 10 once). You may adjust your scores before submitting.

Consider the applicant's:

        Ability to communicate effectively

        Strength of the arguments displayed

        Suitability for the program

        Please place an "X" in the desired box below:

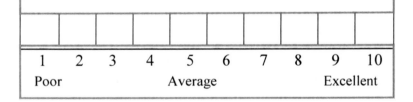

1	2	3	4	5	6	7	8	9	10
Poor				Average				Excellent	

Comments:

Station Notes

-Station 05-

INSTRUCTIONS: You have **two** minutes to read the scenario below. You will have **eight** minutes to complete this station. Please do not enter the room until you are instructed to do so.

As a member of your city's eight member planning committee, unanimous initial support to build a soccer stadium in your city was approved in 2016. However, almost a full year after it was supposed to be ready, construction of the $145-million city funded venue has proved to be tumultuous, marked by lengthy delays and a long list of setbacks that cropped up over the past several years. The reasons for the delays were many. Initially, builders said an unexpectedly harsh winter was to blame. Later, it was revealed that the construction team encountered significant stumbling blocks during the building process: A faulty caulking job in the stands had caused leaks that damaged rooms below, and miscalculations of materials needed in the stands to support the weight of 24,000 spectators meant major, expensive changes mid-build. Several members of the planning committee have now voiced their concerns that there seems to be no consequences for the contractors to finish on time or to give a correct date.

Please discuss with the interviewer how you would proceed in this situation.

Probing Questions

- ✓ Should the contractors experience any repercussions for the delays? If so what should the penalty be?

- ✓ What additional information would you want to seek out?

- ✓ Who should be held most responsible for these delays?

- ✓ Is there anything else you'd like to discuss before we finish?

Sample Score Sheet

Please rate the applicant's overall performance on this station relative to all applicants you are rating. Do not assign a score more than once (ie. if assessing 10 applicants, you may only use a score of 10 once). You may adjust your scores before submitting.

Consider the applicant's:

     Ability to communicate effectively
     Strength of the arguments displayed
     Suitability for the program

Please place an "X" in the desired box below:

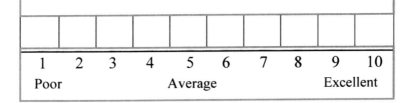

1	2	3	4	5	6	7	8	9	10
Poor				Average					Excellent

Comments:

Station Notes

-Station 06-

Multiple Mini Interview: 1032520112

INSTRUCTIONS: You have **two** minutes to read the scenario below. You will have **eight** minutes to complete this station. Please do not enter the room until you are instructed to do so.

The job is tough and you have fought your way up the ladder of success.   You are working as an assistant manager for a large corporation and have been with the company for three years. The current manager of your department was promoted to her current position two years ago and after her promotion, "the power has gone to her head". She is overly demanding and has a "my way or the highway attitude".   After a meeting, she approaches you and tells you that your job may be in jeopardy unless you can "see things eye to eye" with her.

Please discuss with the interviewer how you would respond in this situation?

Sample Model Response

Interviewer: "Can you please tell me how you would respond to this situation?"

Applicant: "This is a scenario where I'm an assistant manager at a company I've been with for three years and after a meeting, my current manager has approached me and suggested that my job might be in jeopardy. I would first take a step back and ask myself if I might have any personal bias towards my manager that could be contributing to her reaction towards me. After self-reflecting, I would speak to coworkers in my department under the same manager confidentially to see if they have identified any concerns about our manager. Assuming we are all on the same page and concerns are brought up, I would then schedule a private one-on-one meeting with my manager.

During our meeting, I would ask her for clarification regarding the statement that was made about my job being in jeopardy. It is important for me to leave our meeting with a clear understanding of what my manager's concerns are. I would move forward by suggesting that I meet with her regularly to ensure that I am meeting her expectations and addressing concerns. I was involved in a similar situation in a previous job with my manager at the time and I found that meeting regularly allowed me to build a better relationship by communicating with them more frequently and this positively changed my situation at work."

Probing Questions

- ✓ What issues are most relevant to this scenario?

- ✓ If things did not improve at work, would you consider quitting?

- ✓ Is there any role for reporting the manager's behavior to higher authority?

- ✓ What are the risks associated with confronting your manager?

Sample Score Sheet

Please rate the applicant's overall performance on this station relative to all applicants you are rating. Do not assign a score more than once (ie. if assessing 10 applicants, you may only use a score of 10 once). You may adjust your scores before submitting.

Consider the applicant's:

      Ability to communicate effectively

      Strength of the arguments displayed

      Suitability for the program

Please place an "X" in the desired box below:

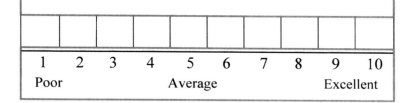

1	2	3	4	5	6	7	8	9	10
Poor				Average					Excellent

Comments:

Station Notes

-Station 07-

INSTRUCTIONS: You have **two** minutes to read the scenario below. You will have **eight** minutes to complete this station. Please do not enter the room until you are instructed to do so.

You are a linguistics expert. Three gods A, B, and C are called, in no particular order, True, False, and Random. True always speaks truly, False always speaks falsely, but whether Random speaks truly or falsely is a completely random matter. The gods understand English, but will answer all questions in their own language, in which the words for yes and no are DA and JA, in some order. You do not know which word means which. Your task is to determine the identities of the gods A, B, and C by asking three yes-no questions. Each question may be directed ONLY to one god.

Please discuss with the interviewer the three questions you would pose to the gods and how you would determine their identities.

Probing Questions

- ✓ What skills and attributes helped you arrive at the Gods' identities?

- ✓ How would you communicate your results to a child versus an adult?

- ✓ Is there anything else you'd like to discuss before we finish?

Sample Score Sheet

Please rate the applicant's overall performance on this station relative to all applicants you are rating. Do not assign a score more than once (ie. if assessing 10 applicants, you may only use a score of 10 once). You may adjust your scores before submitting.

Consider the applicant's:

      Ability to communicate effectively

      Strength of the arguments displayed

      Suitability for the program

Please place an "X" in the desired box below:

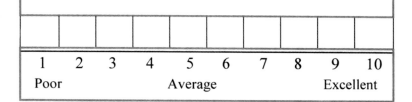

1	2	3	4	5	6	7	8	9	10
Poor				Average				Excellent	

Comments:

Station Notes

-Station 08-

INSTRUCTIONS: You have **two** minutes to read the scenario below. You will have **eight** minutes to complete this station. Please do not enter the room until you are instructed to do so.

Veterinarians must often accept that they will have to provide euthanasia to healthy animals for a variety of different reasons. This contradicts the viewpoint that individuals enter veterinary medicine to save the lives of animals rather than to take lives. Euthanasia of healthy animals is an example of a concern among many practicing veterinarians.

Please discuss with the interviewer whether you support this concern. If applicable, please provide specific strategies to illustrate how you intend to address this concern.

Sample Model Response

Interviewer: "Please discuss with the interviewer whether you agree with this concern."

Applicant: "This scenario highlights the difficult and complex situation surrounding the euthanasia of healthy animals. Unfortunately, veterinarians must often face this dilemma and it contradicts the fact that individuals enter veterinary medicine to save lives rather than to take lives. I agree with the concern raised in the prompt and I would start by gathering information on euthanasia rates at local animal shelters. Assuming that lack of space was the main reason for euthanasia of these animals, I would then explore avenues to reduce the number of animals being taken in and foster avenues that maximize a greater number of animals getting adopted out. We are fortunate to live in a time that supports new opportunities for raising awareness through social media. I would bring attention to the general public regarding the euthanasia of healthy animals in the hopes of educating them on the importance of spay/neuter and adoption programs.

With spay/neuter education, it's important to increase accessibility to low cost/free spay neuter options. I would approach other local veterinarians as well as provide these low cost services at my clinic. For animals already in shelters, my efforts would be centered on finding them forever homes. One strategy for doing so is to promote adopt-a-thons through campaigns on social media. Another strategy to address this concern is to network with other likeminded individuals and work together to maximize our resources. Teamwork has always been an important component of my experiences. When I was a volunteer at our local shelter, several of us often worked together to network and pool our resources in order to find forever homes for urgent pets on death row. In the end, it was tremendously rewarding to see some of these loving, healthy animals escape euthanasia and find their forever homes."

Probing Questions

- ✓ What else might you do to address your concerns?

- ✓ Should euthanizing an otherwise healthy animal be outlawed?

- ✓ What would be the most challenging aspect of veterinary school for you?

- ✓ Is there anything else you'd like to add that we have not covered?

Sample Score Sheet

Please rate the applicant's overall performance on this station relative to all applicants you are rating. Do not assign a score more than once (ie. If assessing 10 applicants, you may only use a score of 10 once). You may adjust your scores before submitting.

Consider the applicant's:

       Ability to communicate effectively

       Strength of the arguments displayed

       Suitability for the program

    Please place an "X" in the desired box below:

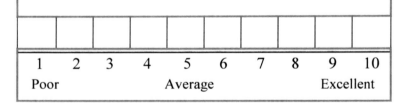

1	2	3	4	5	6	7	8	9	10
Poor				Average					Excellent

Comments:

Station Notes

-Station 09-

Multiple Mini Interview: 131203009

INSTRUCTIONS: You have **two** minutes to read the scenario below. You will have **eight** minutes to complete this station. Please do not enter the room until you are instructed to do so.

The proverbial phrase, "Tell me who your friends are and I'll tell you who you are" is used to represent the idea that like attracts like. A number of schools automatically grant admissions interviews to applicants whose parents are former graduates and alumni of the program. As the newly hired dean of your school, a meeting among the members of the admissions committee has been called to discuss whether the practice of automatically granting legacy interviews to alumni children should continue or cease to exist.

Please discuss with the interviewer whether you feel legacy interviews for alumni children should continue or cease to exist.

Sample Model Response

Interviewer: "Can you please tell me whether such interview practices in the admissions process should continue?"

Applicant: "This is a scenario where I've recently assumed the position of dean at my medical school and a meeting with the admissions committee has been scheduled to discuss a legacy interview policy. Such a complex policy has effects that extend well beyond the program. I would want to start by gathering everyone's input at our meeting and specifically everyone's experiences with legacy cases within our program. Assuming the program maintains admissions data on this select group of applicants, I would review this information critically.

However, at our meeting, I would raise the issue that the current legacy policy should be discontinued because it provides a clear upper hand in the admissions process for select applicants. Afterwards, I would discuss this issue further with the admissions committee, specifically consequences that may arise as a result of discontinuing legacy interviews. This policy may have been overlooked in the past but continuing in the same footsteps would perpetuate principles behind discriminatory policies that medicine has shifted away from. As the dean of my medical school, I would move forward and welcome the opportunity to support an interview policy that improves the chances of admission for all applicants rather than a select few."

Probing Questions

- ✓ Describe the emotions you would feel if your desired outcome was not supported by the other members of the admissions committee.

- ✓ What issues are raised by such legacy interview practices?

- ✓ What would you do to convince the admissions committee to reconsider their decisions?

- ✓ How might legacy interviews affect the quality of the selected student body?

Sample Score Sheet

Please rate the applicant's overall performance on this station relative to all applicants you are rating. Do not assign a score more than once (ie. if assessing 10 applicants, you may only use a score of 10 once). You may adjust your scores before submitting.

Consider the applicant's:

       Ability to communicate effectively

       Strength of the arguments displayed

       Suitability for the program

       Please place an "X" in the desired box below:

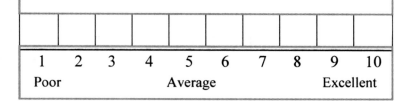

1	2	3	4	5	6	7	8	9	10
Poor				Average				Excellent	

Comments:

Station Notes

-Station 10-

INSTRUCTIONS: You have **two** minutes to read the scenario below. You will have **eight** minutes to complete this station. Please do not enter the room until you are instructed to do so.

You are working with another student together on a presentation for your chemistry course and the grade you receive will be shared by both individuals. You have felt taken advantage of by this student on three separate occasions. They repeatedly show up to the group work sessions unprepared and leave early. Fearing that this behavior will negatively affect your group presentation and overall performance in the course, you schedule a meeting with this student. Your group partner says they will meet you in the library conference room.

Please enter the library conference room and interact with your partner.

Sample Score Sheet

Please rate the applicant's overall performance on this station relative to all applicants you are rating. Do not assign a score more than once (ie. if assessing 10 applicants, you may only use a score of 10 once). You may adjust your scores before submitting.

Consider the applicant's:

        Ability to communicate effectively
        Strength of the arguments displayed
        Suitability for the program

    Please place an "X" in the desired box below:

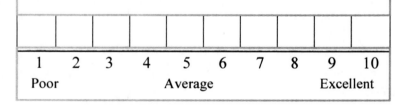

| 1 | 2 | 3 | 4 | 5 | 6 | 7 | 8 | 9 | 10 |
| Poor | | | | Average | | | | Excellent | |

Comments:

Station Notes

-Station 11-

INSTRUCTIONS: You have **two** minutes to read the scenario below. You will have **eight** minutes to complete this station. Please do not enter the room until you are instructed to do so.

A general observation in the pharmaceutical industry is that the consumer costs of prescription medications are significantly higher in the United States (US) compared to other developed countries. A principle to account for the differential cost of prescription medications among developed countries is that the United States bears the largest burden of drug research and development and subsequently must pass this burden on to US consumers.

Please discuss with the interviewer whether you support this principle and the validity of its practice.

Probing Questions

    ✓   Describe the ethical issue(s) raised by this pharmaceutical principle.

    ✓   Please explain what is more important, fairness to the individual or fairness to society?

    ✓   What possible suggestions could you employ to bring down the costs of medications in the United States?

    ✓   What are some possible consequences if the costs of prescription medications continue to rise in the United States?

Sample Score Sheet

Please rate the applicant's overall performance on this station relative to all applicants you are rating. Do not assign a score more than once (ie. if assessing 10 applicants, you may only use a score of 10 once). You may adjust your scores before submitting.

Consider the applicant's:

      Ability to communicate effectively
      Strength of the arguments displayed
      Suitability for the program

    Please place an "X" in the desired box below:

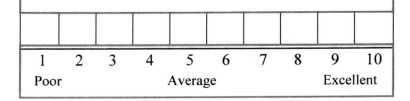

1	2	3	4	5	6	7	8	9	10
Poor				Average				Excellent	

Comments:

Station Notes

-Station 12-

Multiple Mini Interview: 131203017

INSTRUCTIONS: You have **two** minutes to read the scenario below. You will have **eight** minutes to complete this station. Please do not enter the room until you are instructed to do so.

In 2012, the American Academy of Family Physicians published an article exploring the impact of physician role models.   They used scenarios involving physicians offering smoking cessation and lifestyle counseling to their smoking patients.   According to the authors' research, patients have more confidence in preventive health counseling advice from non- smoking physicians compared to their smoking counterparts.   The study also concluded that physicians with medically unhealthy personal lifestyle habits are less likely to counsel their patients about adopting a healthy lifestyle.

Please discuss with the interviewer whether physicians have a duty to act as healthy role models for their patients.

Sample Model Response

Interviewer: "Please discuss with the interviewer whether physicians have a duty to act as healthy role models for their patients."

Applicant: "This scenario provides a glimpse into the important dynamics of the physician-patient relationship. It suggests that a patient's perception of their provider's lifestyle can impact their confidence in following recommended counselling advice. My own belief is that physicians have a duty to act as healthy role models for their patients because actions speak louder than words. While it is theoretically possible for physicians to give professional sound advice about matters they personally do differently, the reality is that patients view physicians with a different eye from 'ordinary' citizens in this appeal. There is considerable healing power in the physician-patient relationship and this may be hindered if a patient's confidence in their physician is disrupted. Working together offers the opportunity to significantly improve the patient's quality of life and health status.

However, from the physician's perspective, their personal autonomy may be in jeopardy if they are unable to make personal choices, consistent with their own beliefs and interests. Despite their personal freedoms being affected, the therapeutic patient-physician alliance involves specific and important physician obligations. I believe many patients understand that physicians are human and when faced with unhealthy lifestyle choices, will require the same help and a supporting environment to change their behavior."

Probing Questions

- ✓ What factors determine whether someone is a role model?

- ✓ What are the implications of unhealthy lifestyle habits such as obesity that readily manifest themselves more easily?

- ✓ What are some possible limitations of the research study conducted?

- ✓ Is a physician obligated by society to take good care of their health?

Sample Score Sheet

Please rate the applicant's overall performance on this station relative to all applicants you are rating. Do not assign a score more than once (ie. if assessing 10 applicants, you may only use a score of 10 once). You may adjust your scores before submitting.

Consider the applicant's:

        Ability to communicate effectively

        Strength of the arguments displayed

        Suitability for the program

Please place an "X" in the desired box below:

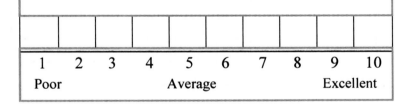

1	2	3	4	5	6	7	8	9	10
Poor				Average					Excellent

Comments:

Station Notes

-Station 13-

INSTRUCTIONS: You have **two** minutes to read the scenario below. You will have **eight** minutes to complete this station. Please do not enter the room until you are instructed to do so.

Multiple sclerosis (MS) is an unpredictable, often disabling disease of the central nervous system that disrupts the flow of information within the brain, and between the brain and body. For 2014, the number of people affected with MS was approximately 3 million. There is currently no cure and most individuals ultimately succumb from respiratory failure. As the current lead researcher, your team has discovered a novel blood test that allows the detection of MS in affected patients at birth, many years before the onset of symptoms and disease are present.

Please discuss with the interviewer your reasons for pursuing such research and the implications of such a test.

Probing Questions

- ✓ Describe the ethical issue(s) raised by this novel blood test.

- ✓ Should parents be allowed to decide at birth whether to raise a child who will grow up to develop MS?

- ✓ What alternatives might you suggest instead of this novel blood test?

- ✓ Is there anything else you'd like to add before we finish this station?

Sample Score Sheet

Please rate the applicant's overall performance on this station relative to all applicants you are rating. Do not assign a score more than once (ie. if assessing 10 applicants, you may only use a score of 10 once). You may adjust your scores before submitting.

Consider the applicant's:
> Ability to communicate effectively
> Strength of the arguments displayed
> Suitability for the program

Please place an "X" in the desired box below:

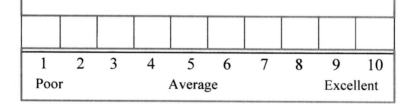

1	2	3	4	5	6	7	8	9	10
Poor				Average				Excellent	

Comments:

Station Notes

-Station 14-

INSTRUCTIONS: You have **two** minutes to read the scenario below. You will have **eight** minutes to complete this station. Please do not enter the room until you are instructed to do so.

The Health Premium (HP) is a component of many provinces' Personal Income Tax system - the revenue generated is applied to health care spending. The HP is based on taxable income for a taxation year. The premium charged ranges from $0 - $900 annually. Currently, individuals with total taxable incomes of less than $20,000 do not have to pay this premium whereas individuals with total taxable incomes of greater than $200,000 have to pay a $900 premium. Research suggests that a disproportionate amount of health care costs result from spending on individuals with taxable incomes of less than $35,000. As the Health Minister, you are asked to respond to a bill that would require everyone to pay an equal premium regardless of their personal income.

Based on the above results, please discuss with the interviewer what will you include in your response?

Sample Model Response

Interviewer: "Please discuss with the interviewer what you will include in your response."

Applicant: "This is a scenario where I'm the Health Minister and legislation has been drafted that would require everyone to pay an equal health premium regardless of their personal income level. As the health minister, my main priority would be to ensure access to health care remains unchanged (or improves) as a result of the implementation of this equal health premium. There is currently a wide range in the current health premium fees paid, depending on one's personal income. A general principle I would try to balance is fairness to individuals and to society. In order to do so, I would enlist the help of my team to gather additional information such as the ratio of the premium to a person's total income this universal flat rate health care premium would place on individuals with personal income levels of less than $20,000. I would also schedule public forums to allow the public to express their support and concerns about implementing an equal health premium.

After taking all of the above into consideration and assuming this flat rate health care premium does not amount to a significant financial burden on individuals with incomes of less than $20,000, I would support this premium. In my experience as a previous employee in health policy, this scenario is one that I can especially relate to. I've dealt with a wide range of policy issues at the local and corporate level and in both instances I was able to advocate for change that helped ensure one's health remained the top priority."

Probing Questions

- ✓ What general principles would you apply to justify your response?

- ✓ Please explain what is more important, fairness to the individual or fairness to society?

- ✓ Is the balance between individual fairness and societal needs different when dealing with the medical profession?

- ✓ Would you ultimately support this bill?

Sample Score Sheet

Please rate the applicant's overall performance on this station relative to all applicants you are rating. Do not assign a score more than once (ie. if assessing 10 applicants, you may only use a score of 10 once). You may adjust your scores before submitting.

Consider the applicant's:

        Ability to communicate effectively
        Strength of the arguments displayed
        Suitability for the program

    Please place an "X" in the desired box below:

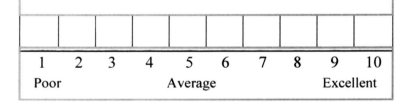

1	2	3	4	5	6	7	8	9	10
Poor				Average				Excellent	

Comments:

Station Notes

-Station 15-

Multiple Mini Interview: 1032520111

INSTRUCTIONS: You have **two** minutes to read the scenario below. You will have **eight** minutes to complete this station. Please do not enter the room until you are instructed to do so.

You are a child support worker for child protection services and receive an anonymous call from a concerned neighbor regarding a case of suspected child abuse. She tells you that a couple and their two younger children, ages 9 and 13, have recently moved into the apartment next door to her. She has noticed several bruises on the children's faces along with poor hygiene. When she questions the children directly in front of their parents, they seem reserved and unwilling to talk and say the bruises are a result of their own carelessness.

Please discuss with the interviewer how you would respond to this call?

Sample Model Response

Interviewer: "Can you please discuss how you would respond to this call?"

Applicant: "This is a scenario where I'm a child support worker and I've received an anonymous call from a concerned neighbor. I would acknowledge to my caller that the safety of the children is my first priority and assess the situation for any signs of immediate danger to them. Assuming no immediate harm is identified, I would need to obtain more background information from this caller about her concerns and the children's environment. I would ask about direct encounters the caller may have had with the children's parents and the frequency of the children's bruises noted. Abuse in any form should never be tolerated and I would do my best to advocate for these children. I would then schedule a personal visit with the family and during this visit I would speak with the children in private.

Assuming that my fears about suspected abuse are validated, I would remove the children from their current environment and place them into a suitable alternative arrangement that minimizes disruption from their everyday routines. I would also engage the help of my colleagues and speak to legal authorities as required by law. In the short term, my response would take these children away from their parents but their safety is my utmost importance and one of my goals by doing so is to minimize adverse long terms outcomes they may experience from abuse. I would also want to support the parents and be a resource to help them towards positive change. In abuse situations, it can be very difficult for the victims to come forth. In my experience as a distress center volunteer, I've dealt with a wide range of abuse within different age groups and I was able to shed some light into their situations by listening to their voices and engaging them to speak about their concerns."

Probing Questions

- ✓ Describe the ethical issue(s) raised by this scenario.

- ✓ Are there any additional individuals you would involve?

- ✓ What are some immediate physical and emotional consequences of abuse?

- ✓ What are some long term physical and emotional consequences of abuse?

Sample Score Sheet

Please rate the applicant's overall performance on this station relative to all applicants you are rating. Do not assign a score more than once (ie. if assessing 10 applicants, you may only use a score of 10 once). You may adjust your scores before submitting.

Consider the applicant's:

      Ability to communicate effectively

      Strength of the arguments displayed

      Suitability for the program

      Please place an "X" in the desired box below:

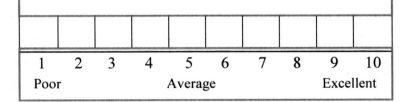

1	2	3	4	5	6	7	8	9	10
Poor				Average				Excellent	

Comments:

Station Notes

-Station 16-

INSTRUCTIONS: You have **two** minutes to read the scenario below. You will have **eight** minutes to complete this station. Please do not enter the room until you are instructed to do so.

Please discuss with the interviewer your decision to pursue a career as a pharmacist.

In your answer, please include any relevant factor(s) that lead to your decision to apply to pharmacy school.

Sample Model Response

Interviewer: "Can you please tell me about your decision to pursue a career as a pharmacist."

Applicant: "My decision to become a pharmacist is the result of all of my experiences. After learning about a few medications in my first aid class, I began to think about health care as a career option and I wanted to explore this further. Over the years, I've sought out experiences in different health professions and enjoyed them to a certain degree but the field that is most satisfying and the best fit for me is pharmacy. Being able to help people is not enough for me. Pharmacists are experts in the composition and knowledge of medications. I want a career that will allow me the flexibility to counsel patients on the drug treatments they are prescribed, as well as be an educator and also have the opportunity to participate in pharmaceutical development.

While volunteering with my local pharmacist, I observe the therapeutic relationship between pharmacists and the patients they counsel. I've also participated in drug development research in my undergrad and this non-clinical aspect of pharmacy was very rewarding for me. These are just a few of the experiences I've sought out which have helped further solidify my decision to apply to pharmacy school and become a pharmacist."

Probing Questions

- ✓ What will you do if you don't get into pharmacy school this year?

- ✓ What do you think is the most challenging aspect to being a pharmacist?

- ✓ What do you think is the most rewarding aspect to being a pharmacist?

- ✓ What do you think is the least rewarding aspect to being a pharmacist?

Sample Score Sheet

Please rate the applicant's overall performance on this station relative to all applicants you are rating. Do not assign a score more than once (ie. if assessing 10 applicants, you may only use a score of 10 once). You may adjust your scores before submitting.

Consider the applicant's:

        Ability to communicate effectively
        Strength of the arguments displayed
        Suitability for the program

Please place an "X" in the desired box below:

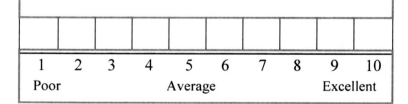

1	2	3	4	5	6	7	8	9	10
Poor				Average				Excellent	

Comments:

Station Notes

-Station 17-

INSTRUCTIONS: You have **two** minutes to read the scenario below. You will have **eight** minutes to complete this station. Please do not enter the room until you are instructed to do so.

Kyle's mother is waiting to see you for a parent-teacher conference. **You are a fifth grade teacher** and Kyle is a student in your class who is struggling academically in all subjects. His frustration threshold is low and you have noticed an increasing number of temper outbursts over the past month. Kyle has not been formally assessed for a learning disability. Informal observation suggests he is reading at a second grade level. He steadfastly refuses to write sentences but loves to draw pictures during art class. Kyle's mother believes the school is responsible for Kyle's learning difficulties.

Please discuss with the interviewer what specific objectives you would have for the parent-teacher conference? In your answer, please include any specific strategies you might use at this conference.

Probing Questions

- ✓ Describe the issues that are most relevant to this station.

- ✓ Are there any individuals you would notify about Kyle's behavior and classroom performance?

- ✓ What possible suggestions could you suggest to Kyle's mother to gain her support?

Sample Score Sheet

Please rate the applicant's overall performance on this station relative to all applicants you are rating. Do not assign a score more than once (ie. if assessing 10 applicants, you may only use a score of 10 once). You may adjust your scores before submitting.

Consider the applicant's:

        Ability to communicate effectively
        Strength of the arguments displayed
        Suitability for the program

Please place an "X" in the desired box below:

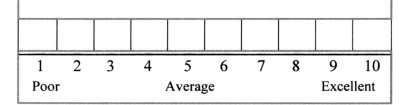

1	2	3	4	5	6	7	8	9	10
Poor				Average					Excellent

Comments:

Station Notes

The following pages are excerpted from the book:

CASPer SIM for the Mind

ADVISOR PREP SERIES

CASPER SIM™
FOR THE MIND

HIGH-YIELD SCENARIOS + ANSWERS

Includes:
Free Full Length
Online CASPer SIM Test

ISBN: 9781944245344

"The CASPer® (Computer-based Assessment for Sampling Personal Characteristics) test is a 90 minute online situation judgment test created by McMaster University in Ontario, Canada and administered commercially numerous times per year by Altus Assessments. The computer based test is taken in a non-proctored environment, raising criticism about its validity.

The evaluation of non-cognitive skills (personal and professional qualities) is a crucial component of any medical school admissions process, and has traditionally been assessed through the submission of personal essays, autobiographical submissions, and interviews. The test was originally established as a screening tool to assess prospective medical school candidates' non-cognitive skills prior to the interview. Applicants are not tested on any explicit subject knowledge and spelling/grammar mistakes are not factored into their results.

CASPer® has been used continuously in the admissions process at the Michael G. DeGroote School of Medicine at McMaster University since 2010 and currently accounts for 32% of an applicant's pre-interview score. It is now a required test at several medical schools, nursing schools, residency programs in Canada and the United States......."

"For the 2017-2018 year, the CASPer® test consists of 12 sections (8 videos, 4 non-video). Each section will contain either a short 1-2 minute video (video-based), or a short prompt (word-based), followed by three open-ended probing questions. The examinee will have a total of five minutes to answer all three questions. There is an optional 15 minute break halfway.

As an applicant you'll never see your actual CASPer® test score but it's still important to be familiar with how the test is graded. Unlike other standardized tests with established pass/fail cutoffs, CASPer® is not a pass/fail test but rather a standardized tool for ranking a large number of applicants based on personal characteristics.

Given the short 5 minute time interval for each section, spelling mistakes and grammar are not explicitly factored into an applicant's score. However, significant spelling mistakes and grammatical errors that take away from the legibility of an answer will in our experience indirectly result in a lower score.

Each section of the test is scored by a different rater using a Likert type scale ranging from 1-9. This means that each completed CASPer® test is ultimately scored by 12 different raters. The raters do not have access to any personal information (such as your name, gender, race, age, etc.). However, the fact that each section of the test is hand scored by a unique rater does make the test more susceptible to rater bias than other computer assessed standardized tests......"

"While each CASPer® rater is provided with the necessary background and theory for each section, the fact that test is hand scored means that there is an element of subjectivity in how your answers are assessed. We will exploit this in more detail in subsequent chapters and in the high-yield sample answers provided in part 3 of this book.

Your final test score is collated from your individual scores, resulting in a maximum total score of 108. Keep in mind that while CASPer® is not designed to be a pass/fail test, the overall outcome is one and the same. Based on our experience, if your total CASPer® score ranks you below the 50th percentile then your chances of admissions decrease significantly."

"Broadly speaking, the test aims to gain insight into an applicant's core situational competency framework by exposing them to hypothetical video scenarios and behavioral word based scenarios. The situational competency framework can be likened to an applicant's ability to display specific roles such as collaborator, communicator, advocate and professional. In additional to these important roles, several personal characteristics most commonly assessed by CASPer® are: **Resiliency, Empathy, Self-Reflection, Integrity and Ethical Reasoning**."

"The following CASPer® pearls are fundamental to achieving success on your CASPer® test. Prior to moving onto part two of this book, please ensure that you have met each objective listed in this chapter.

Pearl 1: Ensure you can type a minimum of 45 words per minute (wpm) with minimal errors.

Objective:

Maintain a typing speed of at least 45 wpm for 90 minutes.

If you're a slow typist, you are already at a significant disadvantage compared to other applicants for this test. With only 5 minutes allotted per section, the clock will work against all slow typists. Typing slowly is a sure recipe for disaster on CASPer®.

Start by determining your typing speed. There are plenty of typing tutorial sites online that will provide you with this information for free. If your typing speed currently falls below 45 wpm, you'll need to devote extra time and practice in order to bring up your typing speed to the desired level..."

Think about a situation where you unexpectedly made a personal sacrifice.

Briefly describe the situation.

What aspect of your personal sacrifice was the *least* appealing to you?

Applying to medical school often requires making sacrifices. How would you handle the situation if you were unsuccessful in your medical school application(s)?

Think about a situation where you unexpectedly made a personal sacrifice.

Briefly describe the situation.

The day I was set to leave New York to attend my best friend's wedding, I received an unexpected call to come into work urgently. I learned that our database system had been hacked. As the lead security specialist for the company, I decided to postpone my flight by 24 hours to stay behind and help patch a security breach and support my fellow team members at this crucial time. In the end, I was still able to attend the wedding and close the loophole.

What aspect of your personal sacrifice was the *least* appealing to you?

The possibility of missing my best friend's wedding was the least appealing to me. This is a once in a life time opportunity. However, in my situation, the unexpected compromise of our customers' sensitive information and my company's reputation required that I place my personal needs aside temporarily and advocate for the greater need of everyone else involved. I'm an individual that works well under pressure and I'm very glad everything worked out!

Applying to medical school often requires making sacrifices. How would you handle the situation if you were unsuccessful in your medical school application(s)?

If unsuccessful, I would use this situation as a learning opportunity for future growth. Becoming a physician is a privilege that needs to be earned. I would self-reflect on my submitted application and seek opportunities to strengthen my reapplication candidacy. Personal growth is also important during this off cycle. I would continue to do the things I enjoy such as travelling, cooking and take on a few new challenges while reapplying to medical school.

Reflect on the most overwhelming situation you have ever encountered in your life.

Briefly describe the most overwhelming situation you have ever encountered.

What did you learn from this overwhelming situation?

What strategies do you use to help you cope when you are feeling overwhelmed?

There are times when it is easier to ignore a behavior than to address it.

Describe a situation you experienced involving a behavior requiring correction that was ignored.

How would you approach an individual whose behavior required correction?

Individuals who fail to address inappropriate behaviors as they arise, display a lack of professionalism. Do you agree or disagree?

"In terms of coaching and practice effects on SJTs, once again, the current literature supports the conclusion that examinees do benefit from test preparation (even for SJTs). One study by Cullen, Sackett and Lievens (2006) examined the coachability of SJTs for consideration as selection instruments in high-stakes testing. Cullen et al. concluded that performance on some SJTs could be enhanced by coaching. In terms of practice effects, Cullen et al. indicated that the retest effects of SJTs are not larger than effects for traditional tests such as cognitive ability tests.

The take home message for applicants required to take SJTs like CASPer® is to be critical and take advantage of resources within their means to optimize their test performance just as they would for other standardized tests such as the MCAT®. Be informed and prepared for your CASPer® test...."

The following pages are excerpted from the book:

BS/MD Essentials for the Mind

ADVISOR PREP® SERIES

BS/MD ESSENTIALS
FOR THE MIND

MANDATES FOR SUCCESS

Includes:
RUC Score to predict your
Interview Probability

ISBN: 9781635878462

"Mandate #3: Choose your high school wisely.

A common question asked by parents is which high school should my child attend if they are interested in a BS/MD program? Many parents believe that sending their child to the most prestigious high school available is the way to go. This may have some positive weight for BS/MD programs located within your own state. However, the pros and cons of attending each high school must be carefully weighed.

In the realm of BS/MD programs, the truth of the matter is your child's high school reputation will not override objective measure such as their grades, overall GPA and standardized test results.

At prestigious high schools, there tends to be a disproportionate amount of students interested in pursuing BS/MD programs from a young age. The personality of these students naturally self-selects for a more "type A" personality which may end up negatively affecting your child's learning environment and ultimately hurt their chances of admissions at BS/MD programs in the following ways: ….."

"Mandate #15: Become familiar with the BS/MD selection process years before you apply.

"There are no shortcuts when it comes to getting into a BS/MD program. These are arguably the most selective programs due to their required time commitment and fierce level of competition. The application process for these programs is typically a year long process that requires submission of many components including personal essays, reference letters, academic transcripts and standardized test scores. During the selection process, admission committees are placing increasing emphasis on an applicant's activities and the history of these experiences.

As a result, it is becoming more difficult to develop a competitive portfolio for these programs without significant advance preparation.

The key elements to be familiar with in the BS/MD selection process years before you apply are: ...."

"Mandate #22: Understand the significance of continuity experiences

An important aspect of any successful BS/MD application lies in the continuity of an applicant's experiences. In the eyes of BS/MD admissions committees, a dedicated and passionate applicant is one who has spent the time and energy to learn about medicine and what it takes to be a compassionate, competent physician. Many parents assume that as long as their child has some physician shadowing and hospital exposure, that they have satisfied the healthcare experience requirements. Unfortunately, we often inform parents and applicants that their healthcare and shadowing volunteer experiences are insufficient because they lack continuity. Continuity experiences in the context of BS/MD admissions refers to ....."

University of Pittsburgh, Guaranteed Admission Program

College	University of Pittsburgh
Medical School	University of Pittsburgh
Program Information	Office of Admissions and Financial Aid admissions@medschool.pitt.edu 412.648.9891 http://www.medadmissions.pitt.edu/admissions-requirements/guaranteed-admissions.php
Program Length	8 years
Application Deadline	November 15
Citizenship	Must be US Citizen or Permanent Resident
Transfer Students	Transfers into the program are not available
Prerequisites	None
Min SAT®	1490
Min ACT®	33
Min GPA	3.90
Number of Spots	Up to 15 student per year
MCAT®	none
Interview	Two personal interviews by invitation
Acceptance	April
Contingencies to start medical school	➢ Maintain an overall GPA of 3.75 with a Biology, Chemistry, Physics and Mathematics (BCPM) GPA of 3.75 as an undergraduate ➢ Complete the undergraduate degree within four years ➢ Continue to gain medically related experience during their undergraduate years

	➢ Seek research opportunities in a medically related field ➢ Seek opportunities for community service ➢ Meet with the Director of the Guaranteed Admit program once every semester to discuss their progress in terms of medically related activities, research and community service. ➢ Meet with the University Pre-Medical Advisor at the start of each semester in order to confirm that they are fulfilling the academic pre-requisites for admission to the University of Pittsburgh, School of Medicine. ➢ Provide the Office of Admissions with an official transcript at the completion of their junior year

2017 Tuition	Instate	Out of State
Undergrad	$17,688	$28,828
Medical School	$52,510	$54,036

Advisor Prep® RUC™ Score

The RUC™ Score for medical school is a proprietary measure used to assess a prospective applicant's competitiveness for receiving an interview invite at their selected program. Using APE algorithms, an individual's RUC Score can be reliably determined. If an applicant's RUC score corresponds to a percent invite probability far below 50%, this ultimately suggests that their qualifications may not be a suitable fit for the given program and that their application may be "screened" out.

To learn more about the RUC™ Score, please visit:

https://apetest.com/edu/ruc/

Enter code: **rucstar** to save **10%** off your RUC Score.

Advisor Prep® BS/MD SnapShot™

APE Advisor Prep®, BS/MD Snapshot provides future applicants and their families with a unique, assessment of their candidacy. Prospective applicants depend on APE to provide high-yield, personalized guidance on their qualifications at specific intervals in time and trust our expertise to prepare them for future success. SnapShot™ is a real time 60 minute one-on-one session delivered with world renowned BS/MD admissions expert, Dr. Kevyn To in person, via phone or Skype and may involve additional members of our team.

To learn more about BS/MD SnapShot™, please visit:

https://apetest.com/edu/bsmd-snapshot/

CPSIA information can be obtained
at www.ICGtesting.com
Printed in the USA
LVOW10s1754281017
554145LV00006B/32/P